TOEIC® L&R TEST
リーディング＆
ヴォキャブラリー
徹底演習

READING AND VOCABULARY TRAINING FOR TH

Satoru FURUYA / Mikako FUJIOKA / Geoffrey TOZER

SANSHUSHA

本書の音声について

各 Unit の【最重要ヴォキャブラリー】の見出し語を収録しています。

🎧 マークで表示しているトラック番号（音声ファイル番号）の左側の奇数番号は、英単語と日本語の意味（太字箇所）を収録しています。

トラック番号（音声ファイル番号）の右側の偶数番号は、英単語のみの音声です。単語の発音を聴いて、後について発音練習をしたり、意味を自分で思い出すなどの練習にご活用いただけます。

はじめに

　本書は、好評をいただいた『READING AND VOCABULARY TRAINING FOR THE TOEIC® TEST』（三修社）の増補改訂版です。Part 6、Part 7 の練習問題を、内容、形式ともに現在実施されている TOEIC® L&R TEST に沿った、よりオーセンティックなものにしました。

　私たちは大学で TOEIC® を教授していて、語彙力が TOEIC® のスコアと大きく関係していることを実感しています。TOEIC® に頻出の語彙の意味を瞬時に理解し、派生語や関連語の知識をどれだけ増やすことができるかが、TOEIC® のスコアだけでなく、TOEIC® 受験のためのモチベーションを保てるかどうかにも影響するケースを多く見てきました。

　そこで本書は前著と同様に、 文法編 と 読解編 に分けて、それぞれをどのように解いたらよいのか、解法のコツを説明しながら、練習問題に含まれている TOEIC® L&R TEST に頻出する語彙も「徹底演習」できるようなスタイルにしました。本書の使用が TOEIC® L&R TEST に向けた学習意欲とスコアのアップにつながることを願っています。

●本書の特徴

文法編：TOEIC® L&R TEST に頻出の文法項目の解法のコツを ここがポイント！ においてわかりやすく説明しています。

読解編：様々なタイプの英文素材の特徴と出題のポイントを取り上げています。短時間で必要な情報を読み取るために、タイプごとに、頻出の問題や読むべき部分を説明しています。

　文法編、読解編ともに、練習問題に取り組みながら、その中に含まれる頻出語彙をピックアップし、「最重要ヴォキャブラリー」として一覧にしてあります。本書では、語彙と意味を読んだ音声も付いていますので、「目で見て意味がわかる語彙力」だけでなく、リスニングパートにも役立つ「耳で聞いて意味がわかる語彙力」の増強も図れるように工夫しました。

●本書の使い方 （ご担当の先生方へ）

　大学などの授業で、半期でも、通年でも使用しやすいように、12 の Unit で構成されています。1 回の授業で 1 つの Unit を学習することも、「文法編」と「読解編」に分けて、2 回の授業で学習することもできます。また、TM には、ご好評いただいた Review Test と毎回の授業で使える語彙テストを完備してありますので、授業のメインテキストとしてだけでなく、副教材や宿題としてもお使いいただけます。

　今回も、前著に引き続き三修社の三井るり子さんに企画の段階から大変お世話になりました。ここに記して、感謝の意を表します。

2021 年 2 月

古家　聡

藤岡美香子

TOEIC® L&R TEST の基礎知識

　TOEIC® は Test of English for International Communication の略称で、アメリカの教育研究機関である ETS（Educational Testing Service）が開発した英語能力テストです。
　TOEIC® L&R TEST（LISTENING AND READING TEST）の問題の構成は次のようになっています。

●リスニング・セクション（約 45 分）

Part 1（写真描写問題）6 問
　写真を見ながら、放送される 4 つの選択肢を聞いて、その場面や状況を最も適切に描写している選択肢を選びます。（放送内容は、問題用紙には印刷されていません。）

Part 2（応答問題）25 問
　英語の質問文を聞いたあと、その応答として読まれる 3 つの選択肢の中から最も適切なものを選びます。（放送内容は、問題用紙には印刷されていません。）

Part 3（会話問題）39 問
　短い会話を聞き、問題用紙に印刷されている 3 つの質問（質問は放送されます）とそれぞれ 4 つの選択肢を読み、最も適切な選択肢を選びます。

Part 4（説明文問題）30 問
　あるテーマについてのやや長めの英文を聞き、問題用紙に印刷されているその内容に関する 3 つの質問（質問は放送されます）とそれぞれ 4 つの選択肢を読み、最も適切な選択肢を選びます。

●リーディング セクション（約 75 分）

Part 5（短文穴埋め問題）30 問
　英文の空所に入れるのに、最も適切な選択肢を 4 つの中から選びます。問われるのは文法と語彙に関する知識です。

Part 6（長文穴埋め問題）16 問
　英語の文書の空所に入れるのに、最も適切な選択肢を 4 つの中から選びます。

Part 7（読解問題）Single Passage：29 問　　Multiple Passage：25 問
　手紙や告知など様々な内容の英文を読み、その内容に関する数問の質問に対してそれぞれ 4 つの選択肢から最も適切なものを選びます。1 つの文章を読んで解答する設問が 29 問、2 つ以上の文章を読んで解答する設問が 25 問あります。

　得点は 5 点刻みで、リスニングが 495 点満点、リーディングが 495 点満点、合計 990 点満点で、受験者にはリスニングとリーディングそれぞれの点数と合計点数が通知されます。

Contents

文法編 ……〔品詞〕

例題

Ms. Brown, the vice-president of Global Inc., has had a very _____ year.

 (A) successfully   (B) successful

 (C) success   (D) succeed

ここがポイント！ 空欄に必要なのは、どんな役割を果たす語？

　英語の単語は、形やその働きによって8つの品詞に分けられますが、その中で「名詞」「動詞」「形容詞」「副詞」の4つを中心に問われるのが、TOEIC の品詞に関する問題です。選択肢には、形のよく似た4つの単語が並び、空欄に必要なものを判断しなければいけません。正解を得るには、①「選択肢の単語の品詞はそれぞれ何なのか」と②「空欄にはどのような働きをする語、つまりどの品詞が必要なのか」の2つの情報が必要です。①については、品詞を特定するヒントとなる語尾のパターンを覚え、②については、各品詞の文の中での役割をしっかり理解しましょう。

　上の問題では、空欄は後ろの year という名詞を修飾していますので、名詞を修飾する働きがある形容詞 (B) successful が空欄には適当ということになります。

正解　(B)

問題文の訳：グローバル社の副社長ブラウン氏にとって、非常にうまくいった1年だった。

　4つの品詞の主な働きと語尾を覚えておきましょう。

名詞　文の中で、主語、目的語、補語になる。

The new <u>employee</u> has five years' <u>experience</u> in business.
　　　　　主語　　　　　　　　　　　　目的語

The problem is his <u>attitude</u>.
　　　　　　　　　　補語

語尾の例

informat<u>ion</u> king<u>dom</u> experi<u>ence</u> accept<u>ance</u> creativ<u>ity</u> neighbor<u>hood</u>

happ<u>iness</u> recov<u>ery</u> partner<u>ship</u> atti<u>tude</u> social<u>ism</u> democr<u>acy</u> soci<u>ology</u>

achieve<u>ment</u> play<u>er</u> supervis<u>or</u> psycholog<u>ist</u> employ<u>ee</u> mechan<u>ic</u> technic<u>ian</u>

動詞　動作や状態を表し、文の述語になる。

We <u>modified</u> the contract at the last meeting.
　　述語

語尾の例

familiar<u>ize</u> streng<u>then</u> re<u>cover</u> modi<u>fy</u> cre<u>ate</u>

形容詞　名詞や代名詞を修飾したり、文の補語になる。

We are trying to maintain our <u>present</u> **prices**.
　　　　　　　　　　　　　　　　　名詞 prices を修飾

The vice-president's comments are very influential.
　　　　　　　　　　　　　　　　　　補語

語尾の例

passionate obvi<u>ous</u> norma<u>l</u> interestin<u>g</u> memorab<u>le</u> sensib<u>le</u> childi<u>sh</u>
juveni<u>le</u> rain<u>y</u> atom<u>ic</u> medica<u>l</u> influentia<u>l</u> obligator<u>y</u> care<u>less</u> competiti<u>ve</u>
friend<u>ly</u> carefu<u>l</u>

副詞　動詞、形容詞、他の副詞などを修飾する。

I **read** the manual carefully.
　　　　　　　　　動詞 read を修飾

The information turned out to be completely **wrong**.
　　　　　　　　　　　　　　形容詞 wrong を修飾

The computer system recovered surprisingly **quickly**.
　　　　　　　　　　　　　副詞 quickly を修飾

語尾の例

carefu<u>lly</u> hard<u>ly</u>

最重要ヴォキャブラリー　🔊[01]　🔊[02]

☐ **budget** [bʌ́dʒit] 名「**予算**」 budget deficit は「財政赤字」、budget surplus は「財政黒字」という意味。

☐ **comprehensive** [kàmprihénsiv] 形「**包括的な**」「**総合的な**」 名詞は comprehension [kàmprihénʃən] 「理解（力）」、動詞は comprehend [kàmprihénd]「理解する」、形容詞は comprehensible [kàmprihénsəbl]「わかりやすい」。

☐ **confirm** [kənfə́:rm] 動「**確証する**」「**（予約を）確認する**」 名詞は confirmation [kànfərméiʃən]「証拠」「証言」「確認文書」である。

☐ **consist** [kənsíst] 動「**〜から構成される**」 consist of 〜のように用い、be made up of 〜や be composed of 〜と言い換え可能。

☐ **contract** [kántrækt] 名「**契約**」「**契約書**」 動「**契約する**」 形容詞は contractual [kəntrǽktʃuəl]「契約上の」、副詞は contractually [kəntrǽktʃuəli]「契約によって」がある。

☐ **department** [dipá:rtmənt] 名「**部署**」「**売り場**」 企業により違いもあるが、「部」を department、「課」を section と言うのが一般的で、「部長」は chief[head] of department、または general manager と言うことが多い。

☐ **detail** [dí:teil] 名「**詳細**」「**細部**」 動「**詳述する**」 in detail は「詳しく」という意味の表現。

☐ **duty** [djú:ti] 名「**義務**」「**職務**」「**関税**」 duty-free は形容詞で「免税の」、名詞で「免税品」「免税店」という意味。

☐ **finalize** [fáinəlàiz] 動「**まとめる**」「**仕上げる**」 形容詞は final [fáinl]「最終の」、副詞は finally [fáinəli]「ようやく」「最終的に」。

☐ **HR** 略「**人事部〔課〕**」 human resources [hjú:mən rí:sɔ:rsiz] の短縮形。同意表現に personnel department がある。

☐ **influential** [ìnfluénʃəl] 形「**影響力がある**」 influence [ínfluəns] は動詞で「影響を与える」、名詞で「影響（力）」。

7

- ☐ **latest** [léitist] 形「最新の」「最も遅い」 「最新の」の類義語に new がある。
- ☐ **maintain** [meintéin] 動「維持する」「整備する」 名詞は maintenance [méintənəns]「整備」「維持」。
- ☐ **modify** [mádəfài] 動「修正する」 change と言い換えられることもある。 名詞は modification [màdəfikéiʃən]「修正」「修飾」。
- ☐ **proceed** [prəsíːd] 動「進む」「続ける」 「〜に進む」という場合は proceed to 〜となる。
- ☐ **R&D** 名「研究開発部門」 research and development の略。
- ☐ **request** [rikwést] 名「要望」動「求める」「依頼する」 make a request は、動詞 request とほぼ同意。
- ☐ **secretarial** [sèkrətéəriəl] 形「秘書の」「秘書の仕事に関する」 名詞の secretary [sékrətèri]「秘書」とともに TOEIC に頻出。
- ☐ **security** [sikjúərəti] 名「警備」「安全」（複数形で）「証券」 security market は「証券市場」。secure [sikjúər] は動詞で「確保する」「〜を守る」、形容詞で「安定した」。
- ☐ **subscribe** [səbskráib] 動「定期購読する」 名詞の subscription [səbskrípʃən]「定期購読」、subscriber [səbskráibər]「定期購読者」も TOEIC に頻出。
- ☐ **succeed** [səksíːd] 動「成功する」 名詞は success [səksés]「成功」、形容詞は successful [səksésfəl]「成功した」、副詞は successfully [səksésfəli]「うまく」。
- ☐ **transfer** [trénsfər] 名「転勤」「乗り換え」「振り込み」[trænsfáːr] 動「移る」「移す」 人やモノの移動に広く使える多義語である。
- ☐ **warranty** [wɔ́ːrənti] 名「保証書」「保証」 under warranty は「保証期間中である」という意味。

Let's Try

Part 5　短文穴埋め問題 ···

1. The budget meeting was _____ scheduled at 10 a.m. today, but has been postponed to next Monday.
   - (A) originality
   - (B) originates
   - (C) originally
   - (D) original

2. We need to _____ these plans as soon as possible. Otherwise, we won't be able to meet the project deadline.
   - (A) final
   - (B) finalize
   - (C) finally
   - (D) finality

3. To get a free _____ to our newsletter, *Marketing Today*, send an e-mail to news@marketingtoday.com.
   - (A) subscribe
   - (B) subscriber
   - (C) subscribing
   - (D) subscription

4. Most of our latest products come with a _____ five-year warranty.
   - (A) comprehensive
   - (B) comprehend
   - (C) comprehension
   - (D) comprehensively

5. Mr. Moore has been _____
participating in a series of presentations
since his transfer to the R&D department.

(A) activity

(B) activated

(C) actively

(D) active

Part 6 　長文穴埋め問題 ……………………………………………………

Question 1-4 refer to the following letter.

Mr. Boris Marlowe
313 Queen Street
Wellington
New Zealand

Dear Mr. Marlowe,
I am pleased to confirm our ------- of coding work at IT Solutions. We would like you to start
this coming Monday. When you arrive at the building, the security staff will give you a
key that will give you access to the elevator and the rooms on the second floor. Proceed
to the second floor and report to Jenny Stewart, the section manager, and she will explain
your duties in detail. ------- Holiday pay and sickness benefits are included in the part-time
package. The HR department will ------- on all the details when you -------. I'm looking forward
to meeting you in person.
Sincerely,

Alison Jonson
Chief Technical Officer

---

1. (A) request
(B) demand
(C) offer
(D) position

2. (A) Jenny will meet you at the entrance to the building.
(B) The president will then hand you over to the section chief.
(C) Your duties will consist of secretarial work.
(D) You are contracted to work up to 20 hours a week.

3. (A) add you up
(B) fill you in
(C) give you up
(D) ask you for

4. (A) arrive
(B) will arrive
(C) would arrive
(D) will have arrived

9

例題

245 Acacia Avenue
New Jersey 38241 ← 差出人の住所[所在地]

Ms. Beth Anderson
CEO
Biotech Corp. ← 受取人の住所[所在地]
Franklin Park
New Jersey 24952

March 8 ← 日付

Dear Ms. Anderson: ← 受取人名

　　Recently I saw your advertisement in *Medical Trends* magazine seeking a researcher to work on anti-cancer drugs, and I would like to apply for the position. I believe that my background and experience will enable me to make a significant contribution to your company.

　　I obtained an M.Sc. in Biology from Oxford University two years ago and found a job with Nova Pharmaceuticals in Los Angeles, where I researched medicines to reduce the side-effects of anti-cancer drugs. While there my responsibility was to undertake clinical trials on human volunteers. These trials gave me insights into how medicines behave in the human body. It taught me not to assume that a drug's success in the lab means it will succeed in the real world.

　　One month ago I quit Nova Pharmaceuticals to move to the east coast with my husband following my recent marriage, and I am now looking for similar work here on the east coast. Your advertisement attracted me because it required an applicant with both theoretical and practical knowledge of anti-cancer drugs. Finally, I want to work for this company as it is well-known as a pioneer in this field, and I am eager to be a part of any breakthrough in the fight against cancer.

　　I am attaching my resume with this letter, and hope to hear from you soon.

Sincerely,
Joanna Moore ← 差出人名
Joanna Moore

Q. What is the purpose of this letter?
　(A) To invite Ms. Moore to an interview
　(B) To apply for a research job
　(C) To inquire about the effects of a drug
　(D) To describe a new discovery

ここがポイント！ ビジネスレター理解のカギは、「誰が」「誰に」「なぜ」書いたのか？

　ビジネスレターを、誰が、誰に、なぜ、書いたのかを理解するためには、これらがどこに書かれるかを知っておく必要があります。基本的に、差出人→文書の最後の部分、受取人→ Dear ～の部分（その前に住所や所在地がくる場合もある）、文書が書かれた目的→本文の最初の数行、または最初の段落、にあります。他に、差出人の住所や所属組織名、所在地→右上か一番上の中央部に印刷、日付→右上の差出人住所の下（または左上）、なども知っておきましょう。

　前の例題では、What is the purpose of this letter?「この手紙が書かれた目的は何ですか」と問われています。本文の 1 文目に ... I saw your advertisement in *Medical Trends* magazine seeking a researcher ～ I would like to apply for the position.「研究者募集の広告を『メディカル・トレンド』誌で見て、そのポストに応募したい」とあるので、差出人は (B)「研究職に応募を希望」してこの手紙を書いたと判断できます。

　「誰が」「誰に」「なぜ」書いたのかを問う表現例を覚えておきましょう。

誰が ▶ Who wrote this letter[memo, email, notice]?

誰に ▶ Who is the recipient of the letter[memo, email, notice]?
Who received[will receive] this letter[memo, email, notice]?
For whom is this letter[memo, email, notice] intended?
Whom is this letter[memo, email, notice] aimed at?

なぜ ▶ What is the purpose of this letter[memo, email, notice]?
Why did A write the letter[memo, email, notice]?
Why is A writing to B?

最重要ヴォキャブラリー ◀ 03 ◀ 04

☐ **achieve** [ətʃíːv] 動「達成する」　名詞は achievement [ətʃíːvmənt]「功績」「達成」。

☐ **advertisement** [ædvərtáizmənt] 名「広告」　同意語に advertising [ǽdvərtàiziŋ]、ad [ǽd] がある。動詞は advertise [ǽdvərtàiz]「広告する」。

☐ **assume** [əsjúːm] 動「当然～だと思う」「仮定する」　名詞は assumption [əsʌ́mpʃən]「仮定」「就任」、接続詞は assuming [əsjúːmiŋ]「～と仮定して」。

☐ **award** [əwɔ́ːrd] 動「授与する」名「賞」「賞金」「賞品」　類義語に reward [riwɔ́ːrd]「ほうび」「報酬」、prize [práiz]「賞」「賞品」がある。

☐ **comprise** [kəmpráiz] 動「～から成る」　be comprised of ～も「～から成る」という意味の表現。

☐ **conference** [kɑ́nfərəns] 名「会議」「大会」　「会議」の意味では meeting、「大会」の意味では convention [kənvénʃən] と言い換え可能。

☐ **contribution** [kɑ̀ntrəbjúːʃən] 名「貢献」「寄付金」　make a contribution は、動詞 contribute [kəntríbjuːt]「貢献する」とほぼ同意。

☐ **describe** [diskráib] 動「～の特徴を述べる」「描写する」　名詞は description [diskrípʃən]「記述」「描写」。

☐ **enable** [inéibl] 動「～を可能にする」　enable A to ～で「A が～できるようにする」という意味の表現。関連語に -enabled「～対応の」があり、internet-enabled「インターネット対応の」のように用いる。

☐ **incorporate** [inkɔ́ːrpərèit] 動「取り入れる」「株式会社にする」　関連語に、incorporated [Inc.] [inkɔ́ːrpərèitid]「～社」「～株式会社」がある。

☐ **interview** [íntərvjùː] 名「面接」「会見」動「面接する」　関連語に、名詞の interviewer [íntərvjùːər]

11

「面接官」と interviewee [ìntərvjuːíː]「面接される人」がある。

☐ **means** [míːnz] 名「**手段**」「**方法**」 単複同形の単語。TOEIC では、means of payment [transportation, communication]「支払方法［交通手段、伝達方法］」などの表現が頻出。

☐ **outstanding** [àutstǽndiŋ] 形「**際立った**」「**未払いの**」 「未払いの」の意味では、outstanding debts「未返済の借金」のように用いる。

☐ **pharmaceuticals** [fɑ̀ːrməsúːtikəlz] 名「**製薬会社**」「**医薬品**」 pharmaceutical は形容詞で「製薬の」という意味。

☐ **quit** [kwít] 動「**辞める**」 leave や retire と言い換えられることが多い。

☐ **reduce** [ridjúːs] 動「**減らす**」「**縮小する**」 関連語として、動詞の decrease [dìːkríːs]「減らす」、名詞の reduction [ridʌ́kʃən]「減少」「割引」がある。

☐ **require** [rikwáiər] 動「**必要とする**」「**（法律などが）〜を義務づける**」 「必要とする」の意味では、need [níːd] と言い換え可能。

☐ **responsibility** [rispànsəbíləti] 名「**責任**」「**義務**」 形容詞は responsible [rispánsəbl]「責任のある」。

☐ **significant** [signífikənt] 形「**重要な**」 important とほぼ同意。名詞は significance [signífikəns]「重要性」。

☐ **term** [tə́ːrm] 名「**条件**」「**期間**」「**専門用語**」 TOEIC では「条件」「期間」の意味で使われることが多い。

☐ **undertake** [ʌ̀ndərtéik] 動「**引き受ける**」 名詞は undertaking [ʌ̀ndərtéikiŋ]「事業」「保証」。

Let's Try

Part 7 読解問題 ･･･

Question 1-3 refer to the following letter.

Johnson and Partners
333 West St., Calgary 4210

Dear Professor White,

I attended the recent outstanding talk that you gave in Ottawa at the International Conference on Sustainability. I especially enjoyed your description of the various means of achieving efficient energy use in new buildings, including the use of solar panels on rooftops. I agree that renewable energies are the way of the future.

Our company of architects, Johnson and Partners, are also interested in the efficient use of energy. Recently we were awarded a contract to design a series of eco-friendly buildings here in Calgary for the local government. These will comprise the City Hall, library, leisure center, and other public structures. This contract is important to us because of the high visibility of these buildings. Since they will be visited frequently by members of the public, we intend to incorporate the latest technologies, and we intend the buildings to be a standing advertisement to our ability as a company of architects.

Taking your talk as a starting point, we were wondering if you could come over to our offices and give a lecture to our design team? We would be happy to fit in with your busy research and lecture schedule. If you find that you are able to do this, we would like to

Unit 1
Unit 2
Unit 3
Unit 4
Unit 5
Unit 6
Unit 7
Unit 8
Unit 9
Unit 10
Unit 11
Unit 12

contact you further to discuss terms and conditions.

I look forward to hearing from you soon.

Sincerely,

Dave Johnson

David Johnson

CEO

Johnson and Partners

1. Why did Mr. Johnson write this letter?
   (A) To praise the professor's lectures
   (B) To buy a modern building
   (C) To find out about solar panels
   (D) To request the professor's help

2. What kind of buildings will the company design?
   (A) Low-cost
   (B) Corporate
   (C) Environmentally sound
   (D) Residential

3. Why is the recent building contract important to the company?
   (A) It will be able to showcase its product.
   (B) It wants to support the local government.
   (C) Professor White will see the results of its work.
   (D) It will improve the city of Calgary.

Unit ❷

例題

Everyone in our offices _____ a uniform that features our corporate logo.

    (A) wears   (B) is worn

    (C) are wearing   (D) have worn

ここがポイント！ 空欄に必要なのは、どのような動詞の形？

英語の文は基本的に、「～が、～は」を表す主部と、「～する、～である」のように主部の様子を述べる述部で構成されます。述部の中心となるのは動詞です。例えば、write という動詞には writes, wrote, be written, have written のようにさまざまな形が存在するので、その中で文脈に合う形を選択します。正解を得るには、「主語の数」「主語と述語の関係」「適当な時制」を考える必要があります。

上の問題では、Everyone ～ offices が文の主部、空欄が述語になっています。主部の中で Everyone という単数扱いの語が主語ですので、述語は単数の主語に対応した (A) または (B) に絞られます。(B) は be 動詞＋過去分詞で、「～される」という受動態を表すので文脈に合わないため、(A) wears が空欄には適当ということになります。

正解 (A)

問題文の訳：我々のオフィスでは全員が、会社のロゴが入った制服を着用する。

適当な動詞の形を決定するためのチェック項目をまとめますので、覚えておきましょう。

チェック項目 1 主語は単数なのか、複数なのか。特に、主部が複数の語で構成されている場合、中心となる主語が単数であるか、複数であるかを見極めることが重要。

Only **one** of the people who were interviewed yesterday _____ experience in the industry.

            (A) to have   (B) having   (C) has   (D) have

▊ が主部だが、中心となるのは one で三人称・単数の主語

チェック項目 2 「～する」という能動態と「～される」という受動態（be 動詞＋過去分詞）のどちらが文脈に合うのか。

The full report is quite long, but key points _____ in the final two pages.

    (A) summarize   (B) summarizing   (C) are summarized   (D) have summarized

主部の key points「主要な点」は、「まとめる」のではなく「まとめられる」のである。

チェック項目 3 ＜時を表す語句＞をヒントに、正しい時制（現在・過去・未来）を決める。また、「～してしまった」という完了形（have ＋過去分詞）や「～している最中」を表す進行形（be 動詞＋-ing）がふさわしい文脈ではないかを確認。

The error was noticed **after** Mr. Ferguson _____ in the order to the supply company.

            (A) had sent   (B) sends   (C) has sent   (D) is sending

after ～「～の後」という語から、「間違いに気づく」「注文書を送る」という 2 つの過去の出来事のうち、「注文書を送る」ほうがより古い過去の出来事であると判断できるので、より古い過去の出来事を明確に表す過去完了（had ＋過去分詞）が適当。

最重要ヴォキャブラリー　🔊[05] 🔊[06]

☐ **commute** [kəmjúːt] 動「通勤する」「通学する」 名「通勤」「通学」　commute to ~「~に通勤［通学］する」、commute from ~「~から通勤［通学］する」、commute between A and B［AB 間を通勤［通学］する］のように用いる。

☐ **corporate** [kɔ́ːrpərət] 形「企業の」　名「企業」「法人」　名詞の場合、類義語に corporation [kɔ̀ːrpəréiʃən]、company [kʌ́mpəni] がある。

☐ **due** [djúː] 形「~に予定された」「(当然) 支払われるべき」　TOEIC では、due date「支払い期日」、due to ~「~が原因で」という表現が頻出。

☐ **feature** [fíːtʃər] 動「起用する」「特徴を備える」 名「特徴」「特集」　名詞の場合、類義語に character [kǽriktər]「性格」「特徴」、characteristic [kæ̀riktərístik]「特徴」「特性」、quality [kwɑ́ləti]「性質」「特性」がある。

☐ **frequently** [fríːkwəntli] 副「しばしば」　often と言い換えられることも多い。名詞は frequency [fríːkwənsi]「頻度」「頻発」、形容詞は frequent [fríːkwənt]「頻繁な」。

☐ **immediately** [imíːdiətli] 副「すぐに」　at once と言い換え可能。類義語に、instantly [ínstəntli]「直ちに」があり、こちらのほうが「少しも時間をおかずに」というニュアンスがある。

☐ **inform** [infɔ́ːrm] 動「報告する」　形容詞は informative [infɔ́ːrmətiv]「役に立つ情報を与える」「有益な」で、TOEIC では、プレゼンテーションや報告書を評価する際によく使われる語である。名詞は information [infərméiʃən]「情報」。

☐ **management** [mǽnidʒmənt] 名「経営」「経営陣」　動詞は manage [mǽnidʒ]「経営［運営］する」「何とか~する」、形容詞は manageable [mǽnidʒəbl]「扱いやすい」「処理可能な」。

☐ **measure** [méʒər] 名「対策」「測量」 動「測る」　cost-cutting measures「経費削減策」や emergency measures「緊急措置」などの表現を覚えておこう。

☐ **memorandum** [mèmərǽndəm] 名「覚え書き」「社内連絡」　アクセントの位置と綴りに注意。略して memo という形でも使われる。

☐ **order** [ɔ́ːrdər] 名「注文」「命令」「順序」 動「注文する」「命じる」　place [make] an order は、動詞 order とほぼ同意。

☐ **region** [ríːdʒən] 名「地域」「地方」　類義語に area [ɛ́əriə]「地域」「地方」がある。形容詞は regional [ríːdʒənəl]「地域の」「地方の」。

☐ **supply** [səplái] 名「供給」「ストック」 動「供給する」　名詞の複数形 supplies は「生活必需品」という意味。動詞の類義語に provide [prəváid]「与える」がある。

Let's Try

Part 5　短文穴埋め問題 ···

1. Our staff is smaller now because three people in our department _____ last year.

(A) transferred

(B) transfer

(C) transfers

(D) were transferred

2. The committee members analyzed the complaints that the branches in the region _____ recently from customers.

(A) have received

(B) is receiving

(C) receives

(D) was receiving

3. Fortunately, everyone _____ the building by the time the earthquake struck.

(A) leaves

(B) had left

(C) has left

(D) is left

4. Daniela is one of our best employees and _____ working here for two years.

(A) is

(B) has been

(C) will

(D) has

5. In order to meet the deadline, Ms. White _____ to hire temporary staff for the project.

(A) will force

(B) has forced

(C) was forced

(D) force

Part 6 長文穴埋め問題 ··

Questions 1-4 refer to the following memo.

> **MEMORANDUM**
>
> **TO:** Sales Staff
> **FROM:** Human Resources
> **SUBJECT:** Virus
>
> Due to a recent ------ of a new type of virus, we request that all staff take special care until
> 1.
> further notice. Please make ------ use of the alcohol-based hand gels at the entrance to this
> 2.
> office, and be sure to wash your hands with soap frequently. We encourage staff to wear
> masks while commuting on the train to and from the office. Finally, if you ------ that you
> 3.
> have any symptoms, such as a sore throat, cough, high temperature, or aching joints, please
> inform management by email immediately. There is no need to be a hero and fight on
> despite being sick. ------.
> 4.
> We hope that by taking sensible measures we can beat this new virus.
> Jane Thomas
> HR manager

1. (A) happening

(B) plague

(C) outbreak

(D) news

2. (A) additional

(B) good

(C) the finest

(D) most excellent

3. (A) notice
(B) will notice
(C) are noticing
(D) had noticed

4. (A) You may come to the office as long as you wear a mask.
(B) First, come to the office to talk to the manager.
(C) From tomorrow, the office will be closed until further notice.
(D) Despite good intentions, that will have negative consequences.

Unit 1 / Unit 2 / Unit 3 / Unit 4 / Unit 5 / Unit 6 / Unit 7 / Unit 8 / Unit 9 / Unit 10 / Unit 11 / Unit 12

読解編 ·····〔告知〕

例題

Retirement of CEO ◀ ──── タイトル

James Itoh has announced he is stepping down from his post as CEO of the OWL Pharmaceuticals Corporation after 20 years as president.◀ When he arrived at the company, OWL was in trouble, with large debts and little innovative talent to create new products. All this was in addition to a downturn in the market. ◀

【James Itoh ... as president.】最初の文で告知内容の概要を紹介 ←詳細情報：役職名、勤続年数

詳細情報：就任時の状態

Within a few years, Mr. Itoh had turned the company around. He laid off numerous staff and asked several members of the board to resign. He also brought in some new people from other companies to restructure the divisions. ◀

詳細情報：改革の手段

Soon the company was making new products, and back to profitability. Mr. Itoh said, "It isn't easy being a CEO. You have to make difficult decisions rapidly. It can be a lonely job, but it is also very rewarding."

So now that Mr. Itoh is retiring, will he sit back and relax? Not a bit of it. He is planning to spend his free time doing volunteer work for charities, and is already planning a fundraising campaign to help eliminate diabetes. ◀

詳細情報：退職後の計画

Q. What is the purpose of this notice?
(A) To advertise a new product
(B) To announce that Mr. Itoh will leave the company
(C) To explain changes of business hours
(D) To tell that the CEO will get medical treatment

ここがポイント！ 「告知の概要」と「詳細情報」を効率よく読み取ろう。

notice や announcement と言われる「告知」「掲示」の文は、製品、人事、ビジネス展開など新しい事柄の導入、従来のものの変更通知、講演会、コンサート、工事などのイベントの案内、求人案内な

ど、多岐にわたります。しかし、設問は、告知の内容や対象者といった「告知の概要」と日付、価格、地名など「詳細情報」に関するものがほとんどです。「告知の概要」は、タイトルや本文の最初の数文で述べられることが多く、「詳細情報」は、文章中に点在していることが多くなっています。

　上の例題では、What is the purpose of this notice?「この告知文の目的は何ですか」と問われています。告知文の目的は、「告知の概要」で示されていると考えられるので、タイトルや本文の最初に注目します。まずタイトルに Retirement of CEO「最高経営責任者の退職」、そして1文目に James Itoh has announced he is stepping down from his post as CEO ...「ジェームズ・イトウが最高経営責任者の職を辞すると発表した」とあるので、(B)「イトウ氏が会社を退職するという発表」がこの文書の目的であると判断できます。

　以下に、「告知の概要」「対象者」「詳細情報」を効率よく読み取るポイントをまとめておきます。

【告知の概要】　文章のタイトルや初めの部分に書かれている。

　　設問例：What is the purpose of this notice[announcement]?
　　　　　　What is true about this notice[announcement]?
　　　　　　According to this notice[announcement], which of the following is true?

【対象者】　内容から類推する場合もあるし、初めの部分に明確に書かれていることもある。

　　設問例：Who would be interested in this notice[announcement]?
　　　　　　Where can this notice[announcement] be found?
　　　　　　Where might you find this notice[announcement]?

【詳細情報】　先に設問に目を通し、読み取るべき情報を明確にした上で、キーワードを手がかりに書かれている所を探し、前後を丁寧に読もう。

・対象者に求められている行動

　　設問例：What should ～ do with ...?
　　　　　　What will ～ have to do?

・詳細な情報（日時、価格、色、地名、部署名、手段など）

最重要ヴォキャブラリー　　　🔊07　🔊08

☐ **analytical** [ǽnəlítikəl] 形「分析的な」「分析の」　名詞は analysis [ənǽləsis]「分析」。

☐ **announce** [ənáuns] 動「発表する」　名詞は announcement [ənáunsmənt]「発表」「告知」。

☐ **coordinate** [kouɔ́ːrdənèit] 動「調整する」「組織する」　イギリス英語では、co-ordinate とも綴る。

☐ **create** [kriéit] 動「創造する」　名詞は creation [kriéiʃən]「創造」「作品」、形容詞は creative [kriéitiv]「創造的な」。

☐ **debt** [dét] 名「借金」　b は発音しない点に注意。be in debt「借金している」、pay off a debt「借金を返済する」も覚えておきたい。

☐ **division** [divíʒən] 名「分配」「部門」　「部門」の意味の同意語に section [sékʃən] がある。動詞は divide [diváid]「分ける」。

☐ **downturn** [dáuntə̀ːrn] 名「景気後退」「落ち込み」　関連語に、recession [riséʃən]「景気後退」や depression [dipréʃən]「不景気」がある。反意語は upturn [ʌ̀ptə́ːrn]「景気好転」「回復」。

☐ **eliminate** [ilímənèit] 動「取り除く」「除外する」　同意の表現に get rid of ～ がある。名詞は elimination [ilìmənéiʃən]「除去」「排除」。

☐ **expert** [ékspəːrt] 名「**専門家**」形「**熟練した**」 関連語の名詞 expertise [èkspərtíːz]「専門知識」も TOEIC に頻出。

☐ **explain** [ikspléin] 動「**説明する**」 Let me explain.「説明しましょう」は、事情の説明を始める際の慣用句。名詞は explanation [èksplənéiʃən]「説明」「解説」。

☐ **explore** [iksplɔ́ːr] 動「**検討する**」「**探る**」 「検討する」の意味の同意語に、consider [kənsídər]、investigate [invéstəgèit] がある。名詞は exploration [èkspləréiʃən]「探検」「調査」。

☐ **fundraising** [fándrèiziŋ] 名「**資金集め**」 一般的に、慈善活動や政治活動のための資金集めに用いる表現である。

☐ **handle** [hǽndl] 動「**処理する**」「**取り扱う**」「**操作する**」 「処理する」「取り扱う」という意味の場合、deal with ～と言い換え可能。

☐ **innovative** [ínəvèitiv] 形「**革新的な**」 動詞は innovate [ínəvèit]「刷新する」、名詞は innovation [ìnəvéiʃən]「革新」「新制度」。

☐ **million** [míljən] 名「**100 万**」 three million「300 万」のように、数詞の後でも単数形で用いるのが普通である。関連語に、billion [bíljən]「10 億」がある。

☐ **numerous** [njúːmərəs] 形「**非常に多くの**」 数えられる名詞にも、数えられない名詞にも付く。

☐ **product** [prádʌkt] 名「**製品**」「**結果**」 動詞は produce [prədjúːs]「生産する」、形容詞は productive [prədʌ́ktiv]「生産力のある」「効果的な」。関連語に、名詞の production [prədʌ́kʃən]「生産」がある。

☐ **profitability** [pràfitəbíləti] 名「**収益性**」 形容詞は profitable [práfitəbl]「利益になる」。

☐ **qualification** [kwàləfikéiʃən] 名「**資格**」「**能力**」 動詞は qualify [kwáləfài]「資格がある」「資格を与える」。

☐ **rapidly** [rǽpidli] 副「**速く**」「**急いで**」 同意語に quickly [kwíkli] がある。

☐ **restructure** [rìstrʌ́ktʃər] 動「**再編成する**」「**構造改革する**」 組織や制度に対して用いる語で、日本語のように「～をリストラする」「リストラされる」という意味では用いない。

☐ **rewarding** [riwɔ́ːrdiŋ] 形「**やりがいがある**」「**報われる**」 reward [riwɔ́ːrd] は名詞で「ほうび」「報酬」、動詞で「報酬を与える」「報いる」という意味。

☐ **segment** [ségmənt] 名「**区切り**」「**部分**」 [ségment | segmént] 動「**分割する**」 動詞の場合、後ろにアクセントをおく場合もある。

☐ **strategy** [strǽtədʒi] 名「**戦略**」 marketing strategy「マーケティング戦略」、business strategy「経営戦略」、economic strategy「経済戦略」などの表現が TOEIC に頻出。

☐ **successful** [səksésfəl] 形「**成功した**」 動詞は succeed [səksíːd]「成功する」「後を継ぐ」、名詞は success [səksés]「成功」。「後を継ぐ」という意味の関連語に、名詞の successor [səksésər]「後継者」がある。

☐ **supervise** [súːpərvàiz] 動「**監督する**」「**指揮する**」 関連語に、名詞の supervision [sùːpərvíʒən]「管理」「監督」、supervisor [súːpərvàizər]「監督者」「上司」がある。

☐ **treatment** [tríːtmənt] 名「**治療**」「**待遇**」「**取扱い**」 動詞は treat [tríːt]「扱う」「治療する」「ごちそうする」。

Unit 1　Unit 2　Unit 3　Unit 4　Unit 5　Unit 6　Unit 7　Unit 8　Unit 9　Unit 10　Unit 11　Unit 12

Let's Try

Part 7 読解問題 ···

Questions 1-4 refer to the following announcement.

Marketing Manager

Company background
3D Printing Inc. was established in 2012 with six employees and $2 million in capital to explore the potential for 3D printing. Since that time we have expanded rapidly and now have more than 50 employees. Our flagship product, the "3D Printer Pro," is selling well. We need a marketing manager to handle the sales strategies for this product on the west coast.

Responsibilities
The marketing manager's responsibilities are to supervise sales strategy in the segment from Seattle to Los Angeles. The manager will be expected to:

Travel between branch offices regularly to coordinate with branch staff
Identify and evaluate market opportunities
Prepare and give presentations to clients
Keep up to date with the latest research

Professional experience and personal qualities
The ideal candidate will have the following qualifications:

2-4 years' experience as a marketing manager
Strong analytical skills

Educational background
The successful candidate should hold an MA degree in marketing, and an MBA will be a significant advantage. Apply by sending an email with resume to Alice Abbott, CEO, at Abbott@3DPrinting.com

1. What is true about this company?
   (A) It was founded a decade ago.
   (B) It has six employees.
   (C) It has $20 million in capital.
   (D) It is growing quickly.

2. Why does the company need a marketing manager?
   (A) To handle sales nationwide
   (B) To supervise the east coast
   (C) To handle new products
   (D) To promote a printer

3. What will the manager's duties NOT include?
   (A) Researching
   (B) Presenting
   (C) Traveling
   (D) Analyzing

4. Who would be the best candidate?
   (A) An experienced salesperson
   (B) An analytical businessperson
   (C) A research scientist
   (D) A veteran marketing expert

Unit ③

文法編……〔動詞の形２〕

例題

Mr. Brown has requested that sales representatives _____ their customers' telephone calls within 48 hours.

　　(A) returned　　　(B) returning　　　(C) return　　　(D) to return

ここがポイント！　適当な動詞の形を決めるために必要なその他のルールとは？

　Unit 2 で、空欄に必要な動詞の形を決めるために「主語の数」「主語と述語の関係」「適当な時制」を考えることを紹介しました。しかし、TOEIC の動詞の形に関する問題では、それ以外に、覚えておきたい動詞の形に関するルールがあります。これらは、知らなければ正解を得ることが難しいルールや知っていると素早く正解を得られるルールと言っていいでしょう。

　上の問題では、主節の中に request「要求する」という動詞が使われています。この場合、that 節の中の動詞は（should ＋）原形になる、そして、その should は省略される場合があるというルールがありますので、(C) return が空欄には適当ということになります。

正解　(C)

問題文の訳：ブラウン氏は、顧客からの電話には 48 時間以内に返事をするよう、販売員たちに求めた。

　適当な動詞の形を決定するために「知っておくべきルール」をまとめます。

ルール１　　主節の中に〈要求〉〈命令〉〈提案〉〈主張〉を表す動詞や、〈当然〉〈必要〉を表す形容詞がある場合、that 節内の動詞は（should ＋）原形を用いる。

We recommend that passengers (should) **take** all their belongings with them.

It's essential that we (should) submit necessary documents by the deadline.

該当する動詞の例

demand　insist　propose　recommend　request　require　suggest　urge

該当する形容詞の例

essential　important　mandatory　necessary　urgent　vital

ルール２　　〈条件〉や〈時〉を表す副詞節の中では、未来のことは現在形、未来完了で表すべき内容は現在完了を用いる。

If he doesn't come within 5 minutes, we will start the meeting without him.

Please let me know **when** you have finished revising the papers.

ルール３　　2 語で構成され、助動詞の働きをする **used to** ~「~したものだった」、**have to** ~、**ought to** ~「~すべきだ」がある。

We used to communicate with overseas offices by fax before e-meil became common.

I have to leave for a departmental meeting now.

All the staff members ought to attend the meeting.

ルール4 過去分詞、現在分詞、to ～だけでは、主節の述語になることはできない。

The plumber _____ that the flooding was caused by improper installation of drainpipes.

(A) to determine　(B) determined　(C) determination　(D) determining

→このルールと determination は名詞という知識があれば、正解は (B) determined に決定できる。

ルール5 命令文に主語はなく、動詞の原形で始まる。

Please _____ to the vacation policy before submitting your request for time off.

(A) refer　(B) refers　(C) referred　(D) referring

→このルールを知っていると、正解は (A) refer に決定できる。

最重要ヴォキャブラリー　◀09 ◀10

☐ **advancement** [ædvǽnsmənt] 名「昇進」「進歩」　動詞は advance [ædvǽns]「進める」「昇進させる」で、opportunities for career advancement と言うと「昇進の機会」。

☐ **allowance** [əláuəns] 名「手当」「許容量」　housing allowance は「住宅手当」、travel allowance は「通勤手当」という意味。動詞は allow [əláu]「許可する」「可能にする」。

☐ **application** [æpləkéiʃən] 名「申し込み」「応募書類」　関連語に、名詞の applicant [ǽplikənt]「志願者」「応募者」、動詞の apply [əplái]「申し込む」「適用される」がある。TOEIC では、applicant は candidate [kǽndidèit] と言い換えられることがある。

☐ **branch** [bræntʃ] 名「支店」「支社」「支部」　branch office とも言う。これと対になるのは main office や headquarters [hédkwɔːrtərz]「本店」「本社」「本部」である。

☐ **commitment** [kəmítmənt] 名「約束」「関与」「義務」　動詞は commit「関わり合いになる」「犯す」「確約する」で、commit a crime は「犯罪を犯す」、commit suicide は「自殺する」という意味。

☐ **compensate** [kámpənsèit] 動「埋め合わせする」「補償する」　名詞は compensation [kàmpənséiʃən]「報酬」「賠償金」で、in compensation は「賠償金として」、compensation package は「一括報酬」という意味。

☐ **correspondence** [kɔ̀ːrəspándəns] 名「通信」「一致」　business correspondence は「商用文」、personal correspondence は「信書」という意味。動詞は correspond [kɔ̀ːrəspánd]「一致する」「文通する」。

☐ **demonstrate** [démənstrèit] 動「証明する」「実演する」　同意語に show がある。名詞は demonstration [dèmənstréiʃən]「デモ」「実演」「証明」。

☐ **environment** [inváiərənmənt] 名「自然環境」「生活環境」　類義語に、surroundings [səráundiŋz]「環境」「周囲の状況」がある。形容詞は environmental [invàiərənméntl]「環境の」。

☐ **insist** [insíst] 動「主張する」　if you insist は「それほど言うのであれば」「お言葉に甘えて」という意味。名詞は insistence [insístəns]「主張」「しつこさ」。

☐ **mandatory** [mǽndətɔ̀ːri] 形「必須の」「強制的な」　同意語に compulsory [kəmpʌ́lsəri] や obligatory [əblígətɔ̀ːri] がある。

☐ **plumber** [plʌ́mər] 名「配管工」　TOEIC に頻出の職業の1つ。b は発音しないことに注意。

☐ **preservation** [prèzərvéiʃən] 名「保護」「保存」「維持」　state of preservation は「保存状態」という意味。動詞は preserve [prizə́ːrv]「保護する」「保存する」「維持する」。

☐ **promotion** [prəmóuʃən] 名「昇進」「販売促進」　関連語に、(pay) raise [réiz]「昇給」があり、どちらも TOEIC には頻出。動詞は promote [prəmóut]「昇進させる」「販売促進する」。

☐ **refer** [rifə́ːr] 動「言及する」「参照する」　名詞は reference [réfərəns]「言及」「参照」「紹介状」で、reference number「問い合わせ番号」や (letter of) reference「（就職先に提出する）人物証明書」などが TOEIC に頻出。

□ **subsidiary** [səbsídièri] 名「子会社」「助成金」「補助金」形「補助的な」 「子会社」の同意語に subsidiary company という表現もある。

□ **transmit** [trænsmít] 動「伝える」「送る」 類義語に send があり、名詞は transmission [trænsmíʃən]「送信」「転送」「放送」である。

□ **urge** [ə́ːrdʒ] 動「熱心に勧める」「力説する」「追い立てる」 形容詞は urgent [ə́ːrdʒənt]「緊急の」「重大な」、名詞は urgency [ə́ːrdʒənsi]「緊急性」。

□ **vital** [váitl] 形「肝心の」「いきいきした」 「肝心の」の類義語に、necessary [nésəsèri]「必要な」、essential [isénʃəl]「必要不可欠な」などがある。名詞は vitality [vaitǽləti]「活力」。

Let's Try

Part 5 短文穴埋め問題 ··

1. If the accountant _____ a mistake, she will not charge us for her time.

(A) makes

(B) will make

(C) had made

(D) make

2. Ms. Chen _____ her vacation plans after her assistant suddenly resigned.

(A) postponing

(B) should be postponed

(C) had to postpone

(D) to postpone

3. Most employees have requested that their paychecks _____ to their homes.

(A) mail

(B) be mailing

(C) mailed

(D) be mailed

4. Eco-Friend Tour _____ a high level of commitment to the preservation of the natural environment.

(A) to demonstrate

(B) demonstrates

(C) are being demonstrated

(D) demonstrating

5. It is essential that all important correspondence _____ by registered mail.

(A) send

(B) sending

(C) sent

(D) be sent

Unit 1　Unit 2　Unit 3　Unit 4　Unit 5　Unit 6　Unit 7　Unit 8　Unit 9　Unit 10　Unit 11　Unit 12

Questions 1-4 refer to the following internal memo.

To: All staff
From: Personnel
Subject: Vacancies at new branch

As you may already have heard, the company is opening a subsidiary in Sydney, Australia, and we are looking for volunteers with good English skill to ------ from our Tokyo branch.
1.
If you speak English and would like to experience working in another country, please ------
2.
your application to HR by the end of the month. ------. Successful applicants from among
3.
those preparing to leave Japan for this minimum period will receive a housing allowance and a higher salary to compensate for the generally higher prices in Australia. ------ career
4.
advancement, we expect the Sydney office to expand rapidly, which will offer opportunities for rapid promotion.
We look forward to receiving your applications.

---

1. (A) locate
   (B) return
   (C) transmit
   (D) transfer

2. (A) apply
   (B) submit
   (C) offer
   (D) hand out

3. (A) The salary and benefits will be the same as for the head office.
   (B) The new Japanese subsidiary is expected to expand quickly.
   (C) Applicants will need to work overseas for at least three years.
   (D) If your English is poor, you can learn the language as you work.

4. (A) In terms of
   (B) With the exception of
   (C) The greater the
   (D) Unfortunately, for

読解編 ·····〔広告〕

例題

This month in *International Traveler*

◆ How to get upgraded to first class on the plane
◆ The best hotels in Southeast Asia
◆ Where to get great deals for designer goods

Apply for our Special Offer!
Purchase a 12 month subscription to
International Traveler today and get a
free travel pillow and pair of "white noise"
headphones.
To get your free gifts, follow
these three easy steps.

Purchase a copy of *International Traveler* online or at your favorite bookstore (price $6.50)
Fill out the application card (found in the center of the magazine or in the "Menu" of the online version)

Mail the card and $20.00 to the address provided, or send an email with credit card details.
Please note that this is a limited time offer. Applications and fees must be received no later than Dec 1st. Offer not available for residents outside of North America.

見出しで広告の概要を紹介

特典の詳細を紹介

詳細情報：特典を受ける方法

詳細情報：金額

詳細情報：方法
詳細情報：金額
詳細情報：申し込み方法

詳細情報：特典の期間

詳細情報：特典の条件

Q. What kind of traveler would enjoy this magazine the most?
  (A) Students
  (B) Budget travelers
  (C) Large families
  (D) People with money

ここがポイント！ イラストや文字の大きさ、書体がヒントになる。

　advertisement「広告」も、Unit 2 で取り上げた告知や掲示以上に、種類や形式が多岐にわたります。しかし、設問は、広告の目的や対象者といった「広告の概要」と価格、サービス提供期間、場所、入手方法など「詳細情報」に関するものがほとんどです。「広告の概要」は、タイトルや本文の最初の数文で述べられることが多く、「詳細情報」は、文章中に点在することが多くなっています。

　上の例題では、What kind of traveler would enjoy this magazine the most?「どのような旅行者

Unit 1 Unit 2 Unit 3 Unit 4 Unit 5 Unit 6 Unit 7 Unit 8 Unit 9 Unit 10 Unit 11 Unit 12

がこの雑誌を最も楽しむでしょうか」と、広告の読み手（対象）が問われています。タイトルの This month in *International Traveler*「今月号の *International Traveler*」の下に、特集内容として 3 点挙がっていて、その中に first class、best hotels、designer goods とあるので、(D)「裕福な人々」がこの雑誌の主な読者であると判断できます。

以下に、「広告の概要」と「詳細情報」を効率よく読み取るポイントをまとめておきます。

`広告の概要`　広告のタイトルや初めの部分に書かれている。イラストや書体、文字の大きさなどで強調されることが多い。

設問例：What is being offered?
　　　　What is the purpose of this advertisement?

`対象者`　内容から類推する場合もあるし、初めの部分に明確に書かれていることもある。

設問例：For whom is this advertisement intended?
　　　　Who is this advertisement aimed at?
　　　　Who can benefit from this offer most?
　　　　Who would be most interested in this advertisement?

`掲載先`　内容や対象者から類推する。

設問例：Where might this advertisement be found?

`詳細な情報`　先に設問に目を通し、読み取るべき情報を明確にした上で、キーワードを手がかりに、書かれている所を探そう。

詳細な情報には、価格、入手可能な期間、場所、方法、条件などがある。

設問によく用いられる表現

（価格、割引）How much 〜、How much discount 〜

（入手可能な期間）When 〜、How long 〜

（入手可能な場所）Where is this item available?

（入手方法）How can customers get 〜?

（入手の条件）　What is a requirement for this service?
　　　　　　　What should someone who is interested in this item do first?

最重要ヴォキャブラリー　🔊[11]　🔊[12]

☐ **banquet** [bǽŋkwit] 名「宴会」「ごちそう」　TOEIC ではしばしば party と言い換えられる。banquet room、banqueting hall は「宴会場」のこと。

☐ **deal** [díːl] 名「取引」「よい待遇」動「分配する」「取り組む」　a great [good] deal of ～は「多くの～」という意味で、後ろには不可算名詞がくる。

☐ **follow** [fálou] 動「後に続く」「従う」「理解する」　多義語なので、一度辞書で確認しよう。as follows は「以下の通り」という意味の慣用句。

☐ **meal** [míːl] 名「食事」　TOEIC では、breakfast、lunch、dinner、supper と言い換えられることも多い。

☐ **mention** [ménʃən] 動「言及する」名「言及」「記載」　Don't mention it.「どういたしまして」は、You're welcome. とほぼ同意の慣用句。

☐ **note** [nóut] 動「～を心に留める」「言及する」名「手紙」「メモ」　Please note that ... は、「～にご注意ください」という意味。

☐ **upgrade** [ʌ̀pgréid] 動「改良する」「(プログラムなどを) 新しいものに入れ替える」「(座席や部屋の) クラスを上げる」　[ʌ́pgrèid] 名「改良」「クラスの格上げ」「(プログラムなどの) アップグレード版」　TOEIC では「(座席や部屋の) クラスを上げる」「ソフトウェアのアップグレード」の意味で用いられることが多い。

☐ **voucher** [váutʃər] 名「引換券」「割引券」　類義語に、coupon [kúːpɑn]「クーポン」「割引券」「引換券」がある。

Let's Try

Questions 1-3 refer to the following advertisement.

LATEST OFFERS AT PERFECT PIZZA

Now it's even cheaper to experience our award-winning pizza! Simply download the offer that appeals to you. Our offers are constantly changing, so if you don't find what you're after, check back again soon.

Please note that these vouchers cannot be used for our delivery service. Terms and conditions apply.

Free drink	**Weekend three-course set menu**	**Discount for students**
Thirsty? Buy one delicious pizza and get a free drink. Valid Monday to Thursday until March 30th.	Have a banquet! Enjoy three courses for $20.00 with our set menu on Saturdays and Sundays until September 23rd.	You can save up to 40% off all meals with a student card. Get yours now to start saving. Offer valid until December 31st.
More for less!	Great value! Save up to 35%!	Exclusive for students!

---

1. Where can customers find these offers?
   (A) In a magazine
   (B) Outside a restaurant
   (C) On a website
   (D) On a poster

2. What condition is mentioned about the vouchers?
   (A) They cannot be used with deliveries.
   (B) They can only be used on weekends.
   (C) The offers end in spring.
   (D) They must be cut out and presented.

3. How can a customer get a free drink with a voucher?
   (A) Buy a pizza
   (B) Present a student card
   (C) Order the set menu
   (D) Arrive on Monday

Unit 4

Unit 1
Unit 2
Unit 3
Unit 4
Unit 5
Unit 6
Unit 7
Unit 8
Unit 9
Unit 10
Unit 11
Unit 12

文法編 ……〔不定詞・動名詞〕

例題

A friend of mine offered ＿＿＿＿＿ us some of his camping equipment.
   (A) lending   (B) to lend   (C) lend   (D) on lending

ここがポイント！ 目的語は、to 不定詞？ それとも動名詞？

　動詞の目的語として「〜すること」が来る場合、動詞によって目的語の形が to 不定詞（to 〜）でなければいけないものと動名詞（-ing）でなければいけないものがあります。例えば、I want to see my supervisor as soon as possible.「私は、上司にできるだけ早く会いたい」で、to see「会うこと」は動詞 want の目的語になっています。動名詞 seeing にも「会うこと」という意味はありますが、使われている動詞が want なので want seeing ... とは言えません。つまり、動詞によって後ろの形が決まるのです。

　上の問題では、空欄は offered「申し出た」という動詞の目的語で、offer は to 不定詞を目的語にする動詞ですので、(B) to lend が空欄には適当ということになります。

正解 (B)

問題文の訳：私の友人が、彼のキャンプ用品を貸そうと申し出てくれた。

　各グループに含まれる主な動詞のリストを提示しますので、覚えておきましょう。

---

to 不定詞（to 〜）のみを目的語にする動詞

＊〈意図〉や〈意欲〉に関係する動詞が多い。

afford「できる」	agree「同意する」	aim「目指す」
arrange「手配する」	attempt「試みる」	choose「選ぶ」
claim「主張する」	decide「決定する」	determine「決心する」
expect「予期する」	fail「しそこなう」	hesitate「ためらう」
hope「望む」	intend「意図する」	learn「〜するようになる」
offer「申し出る」	plan「計画する」	pretend「ふりをする」
refuse「拒否する」	seem「〜に見える」	

動名詞（-ing）のみを目的語にする動詞

＊「やめる」「避ける」「楽しむ」といった意味を表す動詞が多い。

admit「認める」	avoid「避ける」	can't help「せざるえない」
consider「よく考える」	delay「延期する」	deny「否定する」
dislike「嫌う」	enjoy「楽しむ」	finish「終える」
keep「続ける」	mind「いやがる」	miss「しそこなう」
postpone「延期する」	practice「練習する」	quit「やめる」
risk「危険がある」	suggest「提案する」	

remember:
　remember + to 不定詞「～することを覚えている」　remember + 動名詞「～したことを覚えている」
forget:
　forget + to 不定詞「～することを忘れる」　forget + 動名詞「～したことを忘れる」
try:
　try + to 不定詞「～しようと努力する」　try + 動名詞「ためしにやってみる」

最重要ヴォキャブラリー　🔊[13] 🔊[14]

☐ **aim** [éim] 動「狙う」「目指す」 名「照準」「目的」 「目的」の意味では、purpose [pə́:rpəs] とほぼ同意。

☐ **avoid** [əvɔ́id] 動「避ける」 類義語に、escape [iskéip]「逃れる」「逃げる」がある。

☐ **consult** [kənsʌ́lt] 動「相談する」「調べる」 「調べる」の意味では、refer to ～ と同意。名詞は consultation [kὰnsəltéiʃən]「相談」「参照」、consultant [kənsʌ́ltənt]「コンサルタント」「相談役」。

☐ **deny** [dinái] 動「否定する」 名詞は denial [dináiəl]「否定の言葉」「否認」。

☐ **entire** [intáiər] 形「全部の」 類義語に、whole [hóul]「全体の」がある。副詞は entirely [intáiərli]「まったく」「完全に」。

☐ **hesitate** [hézətèit] 動「ためらう」 Don't hesitate to ～は、「遠慮なく～しなさい」という意味。名詞は hesitation [hèzətéiʃən]「ためらい」、形容詞は hesitant [hézətənt]「ためらいがちな」。

☐ **insurance** [inʃúərəns] 名「保険」「保険金（額）」 形「保険の」 「～に保険をかける」という意味の動詞に insure [inʃúər] があるが、have insurance on ～ とも言う。car insurance は「自動車保険」、health insurance は「健康保険」、travel insurance は「旅行保険」を表す。

☐ **investigation** [invèstəgéiʃən] 名「調査」「捜査」 動詞は investigate [invéstəgèit]「調査する」「捜査する」。関連語に、名詞の investigator [invéstigèitər]「調査員」「捜査官」がある。

☐ **itinerary** [aitínərèri] 名「旅程」「旅程表」「旅行案内」 アクセントと発音に注意。

☐ **lend** [lénd] 動「貸す」「貸し付ける」 類義語に、lease [lí:s]「賃借する」「賃貸する」、rent [rént]「賃借する」「賃貸する」がある。

☐ **predict** [pridíkt] 動「予測する」 名詞は prediction [pridíkʃən]「予測」「予言」、形容詞は predictable [pridíktəbl]「予想通りの」「予測可能な」、副詞は predictably [pridíktəbli]「予想通りに」。

☐ **pretend** [priténd] 動「ふりをする」 名詞は pretension [priténʃən]「見せかけ」、形容詞は pretentious [priténʃəs]「仰々しい」「もったいぶった」。

Let's Try

Part 5 短文穴埋め問題 ··

1. The accountant did everything she could to avoid _____ a mistake with the figures.

(A) make

(B) to make

(C) made

(D) making

2. After the scandal was reported in the media, most of the board members refused _____ even though they partly admitted their faults.

(A) resign

(B) to resign

(C) resigned

(D) resigning

3. The consultant suggested _____ an investigation team.

(A) organize

(B) to organize

(C) organizing

(D) organizes

4. I have two proposals that I have to submit by the end of the week, so I can't afford _____ .

(A) relax

(B) to relax

(C) relaxing

(D) relaxed

5. Employees have been considering _____ their supervisor to discuss the current situations of the department.

(A) meeting

(B) to meet

(C) meet

(D) met

Questions 1-4 refer to the following e-mail.

To: Susanna Berman
From: James Rodriguez
Subject: Your trip to Monterey
Date: April 17

Dear Sue,

It's great to hear that you ------- my hometown in a few weeks, and I'm glad you were able to
get some vacation at the end of your business trip. The ------- looks fine for the most part, but
I wonder if we should do fewer things for the first couple of days. -------. We have an entire
week, so there's no need to rush. Before you come, remember to get health insurance and an
ESTA—that's the name of the visa you need to enter the country. I ------- you already know
about these matters, but I just wanted to make sure.

Looking forward to seeing you soon,
James

---

1. (A) will have visited
   (B) visited
   (C) will be visiting
   (D) were visiting

2. (A) course
   (B) diary
   (C) visit
   (D) itinerary

3. (A) It will take you a while to recover
       from jet lag.
   (B) You will need time to prepare for your
       business trip.
   (C) By then, you should have plenty of
       energy.
   (D) There is so much to see that we
       should get started.

4. (A) imagine
   (B) see
   (C) envision
   (D) predict

読解編 ……〔記事・報告書〕

例題

Retail stores turn to new technology ◀────── タイトル

Dull, old-fashioned layouts are disappearing from stores. Retailers have come to understand that their stores must be exciting if they want to keep the attention of the shoppers. One way they are doing this is through the help of technology, especially in-store mobile devices. ◀── 最初の段落で記事の主旨を紹介 For example, tablets and smartphones can be used to take payments, demonstrate products, and offer information.

One prominent retail chain has armed its entire staff with smartphones so they can assist customers and process payments anywhere in the store. ◀─ 【One prominent ... in the store.】主旨を裏付ける具体例1 This practice shortens lines and opens up space. It also helps staff interact with customers more freely. If a staff member can't answer a question, he or she can quickly consult with other staff on the smartphone. Customers can also use some of this ◀── 【This practice shortens ...】具体例1の利点 technology themselves. A leading cosmetics company has put tablet computers in some of its stores so that shoppers can browse products and try on cosmetics by uploading their own photos.

Major retailers are also putting up large, interactive displays that are so interesting that customers forget they are inside a store. ◀─ 【Major retailers ... a store.】主旨を裏付ける具体例2 This may take the form of huge LCD displays that mirror the movement of shoppers as they walk through the store. A major electric car company has even managed to create a stimulating environment for watching cars being serviced and repaired. The service area has a lounge serving free ◀── 【This may take the form ...】具体例2の利点 snacks and coffee, and customers can enjoy watching engineers work on the cars to the sound of the electric motor's quiet whirr. The engineers movements are all displayed on large screens around the store for maximum effect.

Q. Why are retailers using more technology?
- (A) To help with taxes
- (B) To monitor shoppers
- (C) To sell tablets and smartphones
- (D) To attract customers

ここがポイント！ 英文の基本的な構成を理解し、じっくり読むべき部分を絞り込もう。

新聞や雑誌の記事、企業の業績や研究報告書が英文素材として出題される問題は、TOEIC の読解問題の中で、最も難しい問題と言っていいかもしれません。それは、英文が長く、内容や表現が難解な場合が多いからですが、これらの英文は、英語での文章構成の基本に忠実に書かれていることが多く、それを理解していれば、効率よく文章の「主旨」を読み取ることが可能です。英語では、最初の段落、ま

Unit 1　Unit 2　Unit 3　Unit 4　Unit 5　Unit 6　Unit 7　Unit 8　Unit 9　Unit 10　Unit 11　Unit 12

たは１つの段落の中では初めの部分で、最も述べたいことを明示し、その後の段落や文で、その主旨を裏付ける具体例や情報を提示します。ですから、記事や報告書を素材にした問題には、１．最初の段落と各段落の初めの部分を丁寧に読み、何について書かれた文章であるかを把握する。２．設問に目を通し、読み取るべき「詳細情報」が何かを理解する。３．答えを探すために、関連のありそうな段落、箇所を速読する。という３段階で取り組みましょう。

　前ページの例題では、Why are retailers using more technology?「小売店が以前より科学技術を利用している理由」が問われています。第１段落の２〜３文に ... their stores must be exciting if they want to keep the attention of the shoppers. ... through the help of technology ...「買い物客の注意を引き続けるためには、店は魅力的でなければならず、科学技術の助けを借りるのが１つの方法だ」とあるので、(D)「顧客を引き付けるため」が理由であると判断できます。

　以下に、記事・報告書の問題で頻出の設問例を挙げておきます。

【主旨】

　　設問例：What does this article explain?

　　　　　　What is this article mainly about?

　　　　　　What is the best title for this article?

　　　　　　What is the main conclusion of the article?

　　　　　　What claim is made in the article?

【語彙】　「詳細情報」に関する設問の中で、本文中の語句の類義語・同意語を問う問題が特徴的。選択肢を文脈にあてはめて判断することが重要。

　　設問例：Which of the following is closest in meaning to the word "〜"?

　　　　　　The word "〜" in paragraph 1, line 2 is closest in meaning to ...

最重要ヴォキャブラリー　◀15 ◀16

□ **amid** [əmíd] 前「〜の最中に」「〜の中で」　騒ぎや混乱のような抽象的なものにも、人物などの具体的なものにも用いる。「具体的なものの中で」という意味の場合、among と言い換え可能である。

□ **appreciate** [əpríːʃièit] 動「感謝する」「良さを評価する」　I would appreciate it if ... は「〜していただけるとありがたいのですが」という意味の丁寧な依頼の表現。名詞は appreciation [əprìːʃiéiʃən]「感謝」「鑑賞」「評価」。

□ **boost** [búːst] 動「伸ばす」「高める」 名「力添え」「励まし」　動詞の場合、類義語に increase [inkríːs]「増える」「増やす」がある。

□ **conclusion** [kənklúːʒən] 名「結論」「結末」　in conlusion は「最後に」「結論として」という意味。動詞は conclude [kənklúːd]「結論を出す」「〜で終わる」「締結する」、形容詞は conclusive [kənklúːsiv]「決定的な」。

□ **construction** [kənstrʌ́kʃən] 名「建設」「建造物」　under construction「建設中」は TOEIC に頻出の表現。動詞は construct [kənstrʌ́kt]「建設する」、形容詞は constructive [kənstrʌ́ktiv]「建設的な」。

□ **destination** [dèstənéiʃən] 名「目的地」「(品物などの) 送付先」　空港や駅などの表示でよく目にする表現。

□ **device** [diváis] 名「装置」「策略」「手段」　「装置」の意味の類義語に equipment [ikwípmənt]「機器」、「手段」の意味の類義語に method [méθəd]「手段」がある。

□ **effect** [ifékt] 名「影響」「効果」　動詞は affect [əfékt]「影響を与える」、形容詞は effective [iféktiv]「効果的な」「印象的な」、副詞は effectively [iféktivli]「効果的に」「事実上は」。

☐ **entrepreneur** [à:ntrəprəná:r] 名「**起業家**」 会社や事業を始める個人事業主を指す。フランス語由来の語なので、発音に注意。

☐ **maximum** [mǽksəməm] 形「**最大限の**」「**最高の**」名「**最大限**」「**最大量**」 反意語は minimum [mínəməm] 形「最小の」「最低の」名「最小限度」「最小量」で、動詞は maximize [mǽksəmàiz]「最大にする」。

☐ **opposite** [ápəzit] 形「**反対の**」名「**反対のもの**」 位置や方角だけでなく、性質などにも用いる。名詞は opposition [àpəzíʃən]「反対」「対立」。

☐ **prominent** [prámənənt] 形「**著名な**」「**重要な**」「**目立つ**」 prominent figure [fígjər] は「著名人」、prominent role [róul] は「重要な役割」という意味。

☐ **recognize** [rékəgnàiz] 動「**識別する**」「**認める**」 名詞は recognition [rèkəgníʃən]「〜であるとわかること」「認識」「評価」である。動詞と名詞でアクセントの位置が異なることにも注意。

☐ **retail** [rí:teil] 名「**小売り**」 反意語は、wholesale [hóulsèil]「卸売り」。関連語に、retailer [rí:teilər]「小売業者」「小売店」があり、「小売店」の意味では同意表現に retail outlet [shop, store] がある。

Let's Try

Part 7 読解問題 ··

Questions 1-5 refer to the following article.

A Physical Presence Helps E-Commerce Sites Build Their Brands

For years, businesses have been focusing on boosting their online presence to market products and services. But now, some businesses are starting to do the opposite, looking for a physical presence to boost their brand and support online sales. This provides the e-commerce store with the opportunity to show customers who they really are.

Evolve Accessories, a company that makes necklaces, rings, timepieces, and other accessories, is one such company. Run by entrepreneur John Swanson, the company already has a successful e-commerce site, but now the company is opening a 10,000-square-foot retail location in Dallas, Texas. John said, "We wanted to have a flagship destination because we're only online. By creating a destination, we can encourage customers to visit and connect with them on a personal level. The store will be useful even if it fails to make a profit, although of course, I very much hope to make a profit."

John feels that there is another benefit to opening a physical retail store. For a long time, customers had been writing in to ask if there was any way to touch and feel the products before they buy. Now there is, and the customers appreciate the chance to visit, see the products for themselves, and chat to the owner. Amid a growing trend of buying online, people still feel the need to connect with the heart and soul of a store. So while the construction of virtual stores may be skyrocketing, brick and mortar locations still have their place. And John Swanson is a chief who recognizes the powerful role a physical store can play to promote his company.

1. What does this article explain?
   (A) How retail stores are moving online
   (B) Why a physical store is useful
   (C) How customers can shop on the internet
   (D) Why the market for goods is growing

2. What does Evolve Accessories make?
   (A) Flags
   (B) Ships
   (C) Watches
   (D) Presents

3. What happens if the store doesn't make money?
   (A) It can still be successful.
   (B) It will be closed quickly.
   (C) It can be used for another purpose.
   (D) It can be replaced by a smaller store.

4. What can customers do now that they couldn't before?
   (A) Take back faulty products
   (B) Send in typed letters
   (C) Consult with the CEO
   (D) Construct a virtual store

5. In the third paragraph, line 4, the word "trend" is closest in meaning to
   (A) program
   (B) attempt
   (C) challenge
   (D) movement

Unit ⑤

文法編 ……〔使役動詞〕

例題

The conference participants had their suitcases _____ at the hotel before they left for the airport.

    (A) pick up   (B) picking up   (C) picked up   (D) to be picked up

ここがポイント！   目的語は、何かを「する」それとも「される」？

「誰かに〜させる」「あるものが〜されるようにする」という使役動詞に関係する問題も TOEIC には頻出です。使役動詞にも数種類あり、「どの使役動詞なのか」と「目的語と補語にどのような関係が成り立つか」の2つの要素が、補語になる動詞の形を決定します。

上の問題では、使役動詞の have の過去形 had が用いられています。この場合、補語の動詞は原形か過去分詞になります。目的語の their suitcases が「受け取る」のか「受け取られる」のかで、空欄に入る動詞の形が決まります。スーツケースは誰かに「受け取られる」という受け身の関係が成り立ちますので、空欄には過去分詞の (C) picked up が適当ということになります。

正解 (C)

問題文の訳：会議の参加者たちは、空港に向けて出発する前に、ホテルでスーツケースを受け取るようにしてもらった。

主な使役動詞とそれに類する動詞を提示しますので、補語の形とともに覚えておきましょう。

◎目的語と補語の間に、「〜する」という能動の関係が成り立つ場合、補語は原形、「〜される」という受け身の関係が成り立つ場合は、補語は過去分詞。

make/let/have ＋目的語＋（原形、または make / have の場合、過去分詞）

    I had him repair my PC. → 「彼が修理する」→ 補語は原形

    I had my PC repaired. → 「パソコンが修理される」→ 補語は過去分詞

◎目的語と補語の間に、「〜する」という能動の関係が成り立つ場合、補語は to 〜、「〜される」という受け身の関係が成り立つ場合は、補語は過去分詞。

get/cause/force/want ＋目的語＋（to 〜または過去分詞）

    I got him to repair my PC. → 「彼が修理する」→ 補語は to 〜

    I got my PC repaired. → 「パソコンが修理される」→ 補語は過去分詞

最重要ヴォキャブラリー   🔊 17 🔊 18

☐ **deposit** [dipázit] 名「預金」「内金」「敷金」 動「置く」「預ける」 make a deposit は「預金する」という意味で、動詞の deposit「預ける」とほぼ同意。関連語に、動詞の withdraw [wiðdrɔ́ː]「撤退する」「（金を）引き出す」「取り消す」、名詞の withdrawal [wiðdrɔ́ːəl]「撤退」「（金の）引出し」「取り消し」がある。

☐ **expand** [ikspǽnd] 動「拡大する」「拡張する」 TOEIC では、事業の拡大や新分野への進出という状況で使われることが多い。名詞は expansion [ikspǽnʃən]「拡大」「拡張」である。

☐ **household** [háushòuld] 名「世帯」 household economy と言えば「家計」のこと。

☐ **increase** [inkríːs] 動「増える」「増やす」／[ínkriːs] 名「増加」「上昇」 動詞と名詞でアクセントの位

置が異なることに注意。形容詞は increasing [inkríːsiŋ]「増加［増大］しつつある」で、副詞は increasingly [inkríːsiŋli]「ますます」。反意語は、decrease [dikríːs] 動「減る」「低下する」/ [díːkriːs] 名「減少」「低下」。

☐ **issue** [íʃuː] 名「問題」「争点」「発行」「(雑誌などの) ～号」 動「発行する」「支給する」 「問題」の類義語に problem [prábləm] がある。key issue は「最重要問題」、raise an issue は「問題提起する」という意味。

☐ **long-lasting** [lɔ́ːŋlǽstiŋ] 形「長く続く」「長持ちする」 lasting のみでもほぼ同意で、lasting impression [effect, impact]「長く続く印象［効果、影響］」のように使う。

☐ **organization** [ɔ̀ːrgənizéiʃən] 名「組織」「準備」「構造」 動詞は organize [ɔ́ːrgənàiz]「準備する」「組織する」「まとめる」、形容詞は organized [ɔ́ːrgənàizd]「組織的な」「きちんとした」。イギリス英語では、z を s と綴ることにも注意。

☐ **participant** [paːrtísəpənt] 名「参加者」 関連語に、名詞の participation [paːrtìsəpéiʃən]「参加」、動詞の participate [paːrtísəpèit]「参加する」がある。

☐ **regulation** [règjuléiʃən] 名「規則」「規制」 反意語は deregulation [dìːrègjuléiʃən]「規制緩和」。動詞は、regulate [régjulèit]「規制する」「調整する」。

☐ **survey** [sə́ːrvei] 名「調査」/ [sərvéi] 動「調査する」 名詞の survey を用いて「調査する」と言う場合、動詞の conduct [kəndʌ́kt] や carry out を一緒に使う。

Let's Try

Part 5 短文穴埋め問題

1. Ms. Diaz did not get her check automatically _____ into her account.
   (A) deposit
   (B) to deposit
   (C) depositing
   (D) deposited

2. The vice-president had her driver _____ potential clients at the airport.
   (A) picking up
   (B) to pick up
   (C) pick up
   (D) picked up

3. After the new regulation is introduced, the company will not let employees _____ on national holidays.
   (A) work
   (B) to work

   (C) worked
   (D) working

4. Staff at this organization must have all the documents _____ before booking business trips.
   (A) sign
   (B) to sign
   (C) signed
   (D) signing

5. The long-lasting recession in the country made foreign businesses _____ their branches.
   (A) close
   (B) closed
   (C) to close
   (D) closing

Part 6 長文穴埋め問題

Questions 1-4 refer to the following article.

Online Banking Becomes Mainstream

The number of U.S. households banking online reached 40 percent last year. According to a survey by the American Trends magazine, that figure is ------ to increase to more than 50 percent within the next five years.
1.

Young adults with a university education are the most likely to bank online ------ those aged 65 and over are the least likely. Of the latter group, more than 80 percent visit their local bank in person to withdraw money and cash checks.
2.

------. A spokesperson from one prominent bank said:" Having more people bank online means that we can reduce the number of branch offices across the country. This cuts costs and enables us to return money to the customers in the form of ------."
3.
4.

---

1. (A) wished
   (B) thought
   (C) expected
   (D) supposed

2. (A) while
   (B) even though
   (C) because
   (D) since

3. (A) Banks are expanding the number of branches due to demand.
   (B) However, many older people are now used to online banking.
   (C) Banks are actively encouraging online banking to reduce costs.
   (D) One issue with online banking is the extra number of call-staff needed.

4. (A) higher banking charges
   (B) hiring staff
   (C) fewer banking options
   (D) cheaper loans

例題

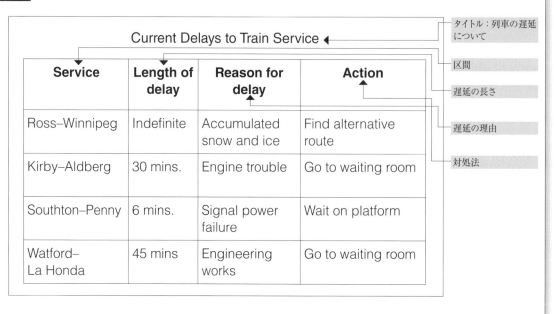

	Current Delays to Train Service		
Service	**Length of delay**	**Reason for delay**	**Action**
Ross–Winnipeg	Indefinite	Accumulated snow and ice	Find alternative route
Kirby–Aldberg	30 mins.	Engine trouble	Go to waiting room
Southton–Penny	6 mins.	Signal power failure	Wait on platform
Watford–La Honda	45 mins	Engineering works	Go to waiting room

タイトル：列車の遅延について

区間

遅延の長さ

遅延の理由

対処法

Q. Which line does NOT have technical problems?

(A) Ross-Winnipeg

(B) Kirby-Aldberg

(C) Southton-Penny

(D) Watford-La Honda

ここがポイント！ とにかく必要な情報のみを拾い読みしよう。

　TOEIC の読解問題では、図表、グラフ、メニュー、スケジュール表、時刻表、旅程表など、文章形式ではない素材も出題されます。これらの素材は、タイトルからどのような種類の文書であるかを理解したら、設問に目を通し、文書の中から必要な情報を探しましょう。「読む」というより「見る」「探す」つもりで取り組みましょう。様々なタイプの文書の問題を解くことが大切です。

　上の例題では、Which line does NOT have technical problems?「技術的な問題のない路線はどこですか」と問われています。Reasons for delay「遅延の理由」の欄を見ると、engine、power、engineering と技術的な問題を表す語句が並んでいますので、それ以外の snow and ice により遅延している (A)「ロス・ウィニペグ間」が正解です。

　TOEIC Part 7 に頻出の図表とそれぞれの必須表現を挙げておきます。

図表のタイプと必須表現

itinerary「旅程表」
　destination「目的地」 depart「出発する」 arrive「到着する」 　accommodations「宿泊先」 via ～「～経由」 transfer「乗り換え」 passenger「乗客」

purchase order (form)「注文書」
item number「商品番号」 description「商品名」 quantity「数量」 subtotal「小計」
total (amount)「合計」 shipping charge「送料」 shipping address「送付先」
method of payment「支払方法」 cash「現金」 personal check「小切手」
expiration date「（クレジットカードの）有効期限」 signature「サイン」

invoice「送付状」 order form と重複する語句が多い。
他に、order number「注文番号」 expected shipping date「発送予定日」
expected arrival date「到着予定日」

voucher[coupon]「クーポン券」
expires ～ [valid through ～]「～まで有効」 for in-store use only「店舗のみで利用可能」
excluding ～「～は対象除外」 cannot be used in ～「～では使用不可」
cannot be combined with any other offers「他の優待券との併用不可」

schedule「プログラム」/ **agenda**「アジェンダ」（セミナーなどの場合）
time「開催時間」 location[place]「開催場所」 presentation[event]「内容」
presenter「発表者」

最重要ヴォキャブラリー　🔊19　🔊20

☐ **accumulate** [əkjúːmjulèit] 動「蓄積する」 形容詞は accumulative [əkjúːmjulèitiv]「累積的な」、名詞は accumulation [əkjùːmjuléiʃən]「蓄積」「累積」。accumulative deficit [défəsit] は「累積赤字」のこと。

☐ **alternative** [ɔːltɔ́ːrnətiv] 形「代わりの」 名「代案」「代替物」 have no alternative は「他に選択肢がない」という意味。動詞は alter [ɔ́ːltər] で、副詞は alternatively [ɔːltɔ́ːrnətivli]「二者択一的に」。

☐ **compare** [kəmpéər] 動「比較する」「例える」 類義語に、contrast [kəntrǽst]「対比させる」がある。名詞は comparison [kəmpǽrisn]「比較」「匹敵」、形容詞は comparative [kəmpǽrətiv]「比較的」「類似した」。

☐ **confidential** [kànfədénʃəl] 形「秘密の」 関連語に、名詞 confidence [kánfədəns]「自信」「秘密」、形容詞 confident [kánfədənt]「自信がある」がある。

☐ **excluding** [iksklúːdiŋ] 前「～を除いて」 反意語は including [inklúːdiŋ]「～を含んで」。名詞は exclusion [iksklúːʒən]「除外」「締め出し」、動詞は exclude [iksklúːd]「除外する」。

☐ **expense** [ikspéns] 名「出費」「経費」 cover expenses は「費用をまかなう」、reimburse expenses は「費用を弁償する」という意味の表現。

☐ **expiration** [èkspəréiʃən] 名「期限切れ」「任期満了」 同意語は expiry [ikspáiəri] で、動詞は expire [ikspáiər]「期限が切れる」。

☐ **indefinite** [indéfənit] 形「（数量、大きさが）不定の」「漠然とした」 反意語は、definite [défənit]「明確な」「確定した」。「漠然とした」の意味の同意語は vague [véig]。

☐ **landlord** [lǽndlɔ̀ːrd] 名「家主」「大家」 類義語に、landlady [lǽndlèidi]「女家主」「（宿泊施設などの）女主人」がある。

☐ **method** [méθəd] 名「方法」「やり方」 類義語に、way [wéi]「方法」、manner [mǽnər]「（個人的な）やり方」、means [míːnz]「手段」がある。

☐ **quantity** [kwántəti] 名「量」「数量」 a large [huge, vast] quantity of ～は、「多量の～」という意味。関連語に、形容詞 quantitative [kwántətèitiv]「数値で表した」、名詞 quality [kwáləti]「質」がある。

☐ **regard** [rigáːrd] 名「注意」「敬意」 動「思う」「見る」 名詞が複数形になると、「よろしくという挨拶」「（手紙での）敬具」という意味になる。Give my regards to ～「～によろしく」は日常会話で頻出の表現。

41

Let's Try

Part 7 読解問題 ···

Questions 1-3 refer to the following letter.

Dear Jack,

Regarding our conversation as to whether we should set up our new office in New York or San Francisco, I have compiled a price index of estimates for various basic items. It's not confidential, so feel free to show it to the other managers.

Regards,

Shelley

Cost of living index for New York City and San Francisco

Item	New York	San Francisco	Difference (%)
Restaurants			
Meal at inexpensive restaurant	$15	$15	0
Three-course meal for two, mid-range	$75	$80	+ 6.7
Meal at fast-food restaurant	$8	$7	-12.5
Basic foodstuffs			
1 kg potatoes	$2.4	$3.4	+43.4
1 kg chicken breasts	$9.5	$13.9	+46.7
500g loaf white bread	$2.7	$3.9	+47.5
Transportation			
One-way ticket (local trains)	$2.5	$2.2	-10.0
Monthly pass	$112.0	$70.0	-37.5
I liter gasoline	$1.0	$1.1	+3.4

Utilities			
Basic (electricity, heating, water) for 80m² apartment	$140.1	$104.7	-25.3
Unlimited data internet	$51.5	$47.7	-7.4
Rent			
1-bedroom downtown apartment	$2,930	$2,787	-4.9
1-bedroom apartment outside city center	$1,798	$1,940	+7.9

1. What items does this table compare?
  (A) Regional spending habits
  (B) Travel-related expenses
  (C) Luxury purchases
  (D) General necessities

2. Why did Shelley create this table?
  (A) To demonstrate that New York is cheaper than San Francisco
  (B) To show which city has the cheapest accommodations
  (C) To help the company make an important decision
  (D) To compare east- and west-coast cities

3. Which categories show the biggest differences?
  (A) Eating out
  (B) Food bought at stores
  (C) Heat, light, water, and connection
  (D) Payment to the landlord

【List on page 42】 Source: Adapted from
http://www.numbeo.com/cost-of-living/compare_cities.jsp?country1=United+States&city1=
New+York%2C+NY&country2=United+States&city2=San+Francisco%2C+CA

Unit 6

文法編 ……〔仮定法〕

例題

The receptionist _____ the vice president if he knew where she was.

    (A) will contact   (B) contact

    (C) contacted   (D) would contact

ここがポイント！ 　事実と異なることを仮定したり、希望する場合に用いる表現は？

　「もし〜であれば」「もし〜であったならば」と現在や過去の事実とは異なる状況を仮定したり、「〜であればいいのに」と希望する場合に用いられるのが〈仮定法過去〉〈仮定法過去完了〉です。状況を設定する if 節の動詞に、現在の事実と異なることを仮定する〈仮定法過去〉の場合は過去形、過去の事実と異なることを仮定する〈仮定法過去完了〉の場合には過去完了形と、1つずつ古い時制を用いるのがポイントです。複雑な印象のある文型ですが、if 節と主節の述語部分の形を理解していれば瞬時に正解を得られる、比較的取り組みやすい問題だと言えます。

　上の問題では、if 節の動詞が knew と過去形ですので、「もし彼女(副社長)の居場所を知っていれば」という意味から、「知らない」という現在の事実と異なることを仮定している〈仮定法過去〉と判断できます。主節の述語部分は〈would ＋動詞の原形〉になりますので、(D) would contact が適当です。

正解　(D)

問題文の訳：受付係は、副社長の居場所を知っていれば、彼女に連絡をするのですが…。

　TOEIC に頻出の〈仮定法過去〉と〈仮定法過去完了〉の形を提示しますので、公式として覚えておきましょう。

仮定法過去　　現在の事実と異なることを仮定する

    If 主語＋動詞の過去形…, 主語＋ would 動詞の原形

    If I **knew** her phone number, I **would call** her immediately.

仮定法過去完了　　過去の事実と異なることを仮定する

    If 主語＋動詞の過去完了形…, 主語＋ would have 過去分詞

    If I **had known** her phone number, I **would have called** her immediately.

最重要ヴォキャブラリー　　　　　　　　　　🔊21　🔊22

☐ **apologize** [əpɑ́lədʒàiz] 動「謝る」 「(人に)〜のことを謝る」と言う場合、apologize to（人）for 〜という形で表現する。

☐ **complete** [kəmplíːt] 動「完了する」「終える」「仕上げる」 形「完全な」 動詞の場合、finish と言い換えることができる。名詞は completion [kəmplíːʃən]「完了。」

☐ **draw** [drɔ́ː] 名「引き分け」「くじ引き」「(対戦の) 組み合わせ抽選」 「くじ引き」の意味では、drawing [drɔ́ːiŋ] と言っても同意である。

☐ **inconvenience** [ìnkənvíːnjəns] 名「不便なこと」「迷惑なこと」 動「迷惑をかける」 形容詞は inconvenient [ìnkənvíːnjənt]「不便な」「迷惑な」である。

☐ **individual** [ìndəvídʒuəl] 名「個人」形「個々の」「個人の」「独特な」 the rights of the individual は「個人の権利」、a very individual style of ～と言うと「非常に個性的な～」という意味。

☐ **labor** [léibər] 名「労働」「労働者」動「働く」 labor and management は「労働者側と経営者」「労使」、labor union は「労働組合」という意味。

☐ **questionnaire** [kwèstʃənέər] 名「アンケート用紙」 綴りとアクセントの位置に注意。「アンケート用紙に記入する」と言う場合は、動詞の complete [kəmplíːt] や fill out[in] などを一緒に用いる。

☐ **raise** [réiz] 名「昇給」動「上げる」「育てる」「集める」 名詞の場合、関連語に promotion [prəmóuʃən]「昇進」「昇格」がある。動詞の場合、非常に多くの意味があるので一度辞書で確認しよう。

☐ **responsive** [rispánsiv] 形「すぐに対応できる」「反応が早い」 反意語は unresponsive [ə̀nrispánsiv]「反応がよくない」。副詞は responsively [rispánsivli]「敏感に」、名詞は responsiveness [rispánsivnis]「敏感さ」である。

☐ **review** [rivjúː] 動「再検討する」名「批評」 re- は「再び」、view は「見る」という意味を持つ。

Let's Try

Part 5 短文穴埋め問題

1. If Central Corporation _____ more available capital, they would have expanded their European operations.

   (A) has

   (B) had had

   (C) were having

   (D) has had

2. If the project _____ more successful, the manager's request for a raise would be reviewed seriously.

   (A) is

   (B) were

   (C) would have been

   (D) has been

3. I _____ for the position if there were more benefits.

   (A) apply

   (B) applied

   (C) would apply

   (D) will apply

4. If management and labor hadn't agreed on the wages, the workers _____ on strike.

   (A) go

   (B) will go

   (C) would have gone

   (D) had gone

5. Without our manager's valuable advice, our project _____ .

   (A) had succeeded

   (B) hadn't succeeded

   (C) will have succeeded

   (D) wouldn't have succeeded

Unit 1
Unit 2
Unit 3
Unit 4
Unit 5
Unit 6
Unit 7
Unit 8
Unit 9
Unit 10
Unit 11
Unit 12

Questions 1-4 refer to the following email.

Dear Customer,

Do you have a few spare minutes right now? We ------ to know how you rate our company
in terms of satisfaction with the products, reliability, and customer service. ------ is your
                                                          1.   2.
opportunity to tell us what you think we do well and how we can improve. Please complete
this questionnaire, and we will include you in our draw for a top prize of $1,000.

All information you provide will be treated ------ and will only be used for research
                                                3.
purposes. Your data will not be linked to you as an individual. We appreciate your great help
in making our company ever more responsive to its customers. ------.
                                                                    4.

Graham Hill,
CEO,
Home Furnishings Inc.

1. (A) like
   (B) will like
   (C) would like
   (D) are liking

2. (A) This
   (B) That
   (C) Then
   (D) There

3. (A) watchfully
   (B) confidentially
   (C) secretly
   (D) thoughtfully

4. (A) We apologize for the inconvenience.
   (B) You can take the test from next week.
   (C) This information be added to your
       profile.
   (D) Good luck in the prize draw!

読解編 ……〔表・グラフ2〕

例題

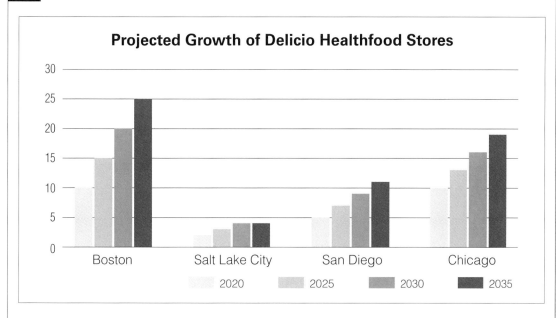

Q. What is the purpose of this graph?
(A) To compare the incomes of four areas
(B) To show past purchase of stores
(C) To indicate future population growth
(D) To suggest the future increase in stores

ここがポイント！ グラフは「タイトル」「縦軸」「横軸」の3か所に注目しよう。

　TOEIC の読解問題では、文章形式ではない様々なタイプの素材が出題されることを Unit 5 で紹介しました。これらの素材では、タイトルから内容を把握し、設問に目を通して、目当ての情報を探す読み方をお勧めしました。中でもグラフは、タイトルを読むことで、ほぼ瞬時に何のグラフであるのかを理解できますし、加えて縦軸と横軸が何を表しているかを注目すると、設問に答えることが可能です。

　上の例題では、What is the purpose of this graph?「このグラフの目的は何か」が問われています。タイトルが Projected Growth of Delicio Healthfood Stores「デリシオ健康食品店の成長予測」ですから、(D)「店舗の将来の成長を示すため」が正解です。

　Unit 5 に引き続き、TOEIC Part 7 に頻出の図表とそれぞれの必須表現を挙げますので、覚えておきましょう。

graph「グラフ」/ **chart**「図表」/ **table**「表」

   survey「調査」   questionnaire「アンケート」

   statistics「統計」   per ～「～当たりの」

   figure「表、数字」   respondent「回答者」

   male「男性」   female「女性」

   age「年齢」

survey[evaluation] form「調査表」

   rating「評点」   satisfied「満足した」

   agree「そう思う」   disagree「そうは思わない」

menu「メニュー」

   appetizer「前菜」   beverage「飲み物」

   closed on ～「店休日」

(weather) forecast「天気予報」

   occasionally「時々」   later「のち」   temperature「気温」

   low=lowest temperature「最低気温」

   high=highest temperature「最高気温」

stock price「株価」

   stock market「株式市場」   bonds「債券」

   low「最安値」   high「最高値」

   close「終値」   change「前日比」

   volume「取引高」

最重要ヴォキャブラリー　　🔊23　🔊24

☐ **beverage** [bévəridʒ] 名 **「飲み物」**　水以外の飲み物を表す。掲示やメニューなどに使われることが多く、口語では drink と言うことが多い。

☐ **bond** [bánd] 名 **「絆」「債券」「束縛」**　TOEIC には「債券」の意味で頻出。government bonds は「国債」、corporate bonds は「社債」、bond market は「債券市場」という意味。

☐ **discover** [diskʌ́vər] 動 **「発見する」「判明する」**　名詞は discovery [diskʌ́vəri]「発見」で、make a discovery で discover と同意である。

☐ **female** [fíːmeil] 形 **「女性の」「雌の」**　反意語は male [méil]「男性の」「雄の」。書類などの性別記入欄では、F（女性）、M（男性）と省略されることもある。

☐ **fluctuate** [flʌ́ktʃuèit] 動 **「上下する」「変動する」**　数値の変動に用いる語なので、TOEIC では株価や金利、物価の変動に用いられることが多い。名詞は、fluctuation [flʌ̀ktʃuéiʃən]「変動」。

☐ **forecast** [fɔ́ːrkæst] 名 **「予想」「予測」** 動 **「予想する」「予測する」**　weather forecast は「天気予報」、sales forecast は「売上予測」という意味。

☐ **growth** [gróuθ] 名 **「増加」「成長」**　economic growth は「経済成長」、annual growth rate は「年間成長率」、rapid [slow] growth は「急速な［緩やかな］成長」という意味。動詞は grow [gróu]「育つ」「増える」。

☐ **last** [læst] 動 **「続く」「長持ちする」**　類義語に、continue [kəntínjuː]「継続する」や persist [pərsíst]「しつこく続ける」「固執する」がある。

☐ **male** [méil] 形 **「男性の」「雄の」**　male-dominated は「男性中心［支配］の」という意味。

☐ **past** [pǽst] 形 **「過去の」「過ぎたばかりの」** 名 **「過去」** 前 **「～を過ぎて」**　関連語に、present [préznt] 形「現在の」名「現在」、future [fjúːtʃər] 形「未来の」「将来の」名「未来」「将来」がある。

☐ **per** [pər] 前 **「～につき」「～当たり」**　per day [week, hour]「1 日［1 週、1 時間］につき」のように用い、per の後ろには a や an などの冠詞をつけないことに注意。

☐ **population** [pàpjuléiʃən] 名 **「人口」**　large [small] population「多い［少ない］人口」のように表現し、many や a few を使わないことに注意しよう。

☐ **productivity** [pròudʌktívəti] 名 **「生産力」「生産性」**　high [low] productivity は「高い［低い］生産性」という意味。形容詞は productive [prədʌ́ktiv]「有意義な」「生産の」、副詞は productively [prədʌ́ktivli]「生産的に」「有意義に」。

☐ **project** [prədʒékt] 動 **「計画する」「予測する」「映し出す」**　「予測する」という意味の同意語に、forecast [fɔ́ːrkæst] や predict [pridíkt] がある。

☐ **respondent** [rispándənt] 名 **「(調査などの) 回答者」**　関連語に、動詞の respond [rispánd]「対応する」「応答する」、名詞の response [rispáns]「反応」「返答」がある。

☐ **statistics** [stətístiks] 名 **「統計」「統計学」**　単数形の場合、「(統計上の) 数値」という意味になる。形容詞は statistical [stətístikəl]「統計に基づく」「統計の」。

Let's Try

Part 7 読解問題 ··

Questions 1-2 refer to the following message.

Jay—I just discovered this sleep app. You put your smartphone on your pillow and it measures your sleep patterns. It's helping me to get a good night's sleep! How about notifying the staff? Some of them might want to try it, and it might increase productivity if they can sleep better. Here's my chart for last night including waking up to take care of the baby. Note that a good chart has a regular pattern lasting for seven hours and fluctuating between light and deep sleep.
All for now, Kay.

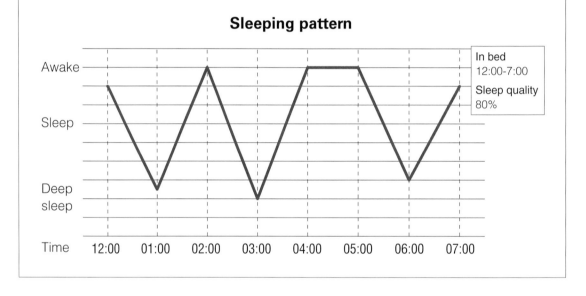

1. What is the purpose of this chart?
   (A) To sleep for seven hours
   (B) To record how a person sleeps
   (C) To repeat waking up and falling asleep
   (D) To get up early in the morning

2. How many hours did Kay spend sleeping?
   (A) 4
   (B) 5
   (C) 6
   (D) 7

文法編 ……〔関係詞〕

例題

The candidate _____ was hired this week will begin training at our headquarters within a month.

(A) which　　　(B) who　　　(C) whose　　　(D) where

ここがポイント！ 「私が買った・本」のように、主語と述語で名詞を修飾することができる！

　Unit 1 で学習したように、形容詞には名詞を修飾する働きがありますが、他に、主語と動詞のある節にも名詞を修飾する働きがあります。この場合、修飾される名詞（＝先行詞）と後にくる修飾節をつなぐ働きをするのが関係代名詞です。関係代名詞も複数あり、「先行詞が人、人以外のもののどちらを表しているか」と「後の修飾節の中でどのような役割をしているか」の2つの要素で、どれを用いるのかが決まります。

　上の問題では、空欄から hired までの部分が前の名詞 The candidate を修飾しています。つまり、先行詞 The candidate「応募者」は〈人〉を表していて、The candidate was hired. のように修飾節の主語になれるので、空欄には主格の関係代名詞 (B) who が適当ということになります。

正解 (B)

問題文の訳：今週採用された応募者は、1 か月以内に本社で研修を開始する。

以下に、基本的な関係代名詞とそれぞれの働きをまとめますので、覚えておきましょう。

先行詞 ＼ 修飾節での役割	主語	所有格「〜の」	目的語
人	who	whose	who[whom]
人以外	which	whose[of which]	which[that]
人と人以外	that		that
先行詞（〜のこと）を含む	what		what

1. who

Ms. Smith is the person **who** is in charge of making an inventory of office supplies.
先行詞 the person は「人」で、the person is in charge of making an inventory ... のように修飾節の主語となるので、関係代名詞 who を用いる。

2. whose[of which]

He gave a presentation **whose title [the title of which]** has slipped my memory.
先行詞 a presentation は「人以外」で、a presentation's title のように「プレゼンテーションのタイトル」と所有の働きをしているので、関係代名詞 whose[〜 of which] を用いる。

3. which[that]

The benefits **which[that]** the company offers are quite attractive to staff members.
先行詞 the benefits は「人以外」で、the company offers the benefits のように修飾節の目的語となるので、関係代名詞は which[that] を用いる。

What surprised us is that the CEO announced his resignation at the press conference.

関係代名詞 what は先行詞 the thing と関係代名詞 which の役割を含んでいると考えるとよい。先行詞の働きも含まれているので、この前には修飾される先行詞となる名詞がないことに注意。

最重要ヴォキャブラリー　　　　　🔊25　🔊26

☐ **coming** [kámiŋ] 形「来るべき」「今度の」「将来性のある」　the coming conference のように、必ず名詞の前に用いる。「今度の」の意味では、upcoming と言い換え可能。

☐ **considerable** [kənsídərəbl] 形「(数や程度が) かなりの」「重要な」　「重要な」の意味では、類義語に important がある。副詞は considerably [kənsídərəbli]「かなり」。

☐ **distributor** [distríbjutər] 名「販売者」「卸業者」　関連語に名詞の distribution [dìstrəbjú:ʃən]「配達」「分配」、動詞の distribute [distríbju:t]「配送する」「分配する」がある。

☐ **export** [ékspɔ:rt] 名「輸出」「輸出品」/ [ikspɔ́:rt] 動「輸出する」　名詞と動詞でアクセントの位置が異なるので、注意。反意語は import [ímpɔ:rt]「輸入」/ [impɔ́:rt]「輸入する」である。

☐ **load** [lóud] 動「積む」名「積荷」　unload [ʌnlóud] は「荷物をおろす」という意味の動詞。un- には、動詞の前に付けて、反対の動作を表す働きがあることを覚えておくとよい。

☐ **officially** [əfíʃəli] 副「公式に」「正式に」「職務上」　反意語は unofficially [ʌ̀nəfíʃəli]「非公式に」、形容詞は official [əfíʃəl]「公式な」「表向きの」。

☐ **pleased** [plí:zd] 形「喜んで」　Pleased to meet you.「初めまして、お目にかかれてうれしいです」は、初対面の人への挨拶として頻出の表現である。

☐ **transport** [trǽnspɔ:rt] 名「交通機関」「輸送」/ [trænspɔ́:rt] 動「運ぶ」　同意語に transportation [trænspərtéiʃən] がある。public transport[transportation] と言えば、「公共交通機関」のこと。

☐ **warehouse** [wéərhàus] 名「倉庫」　ware [wéər] は「商品」「陶器」という意味の名詞で、それらを保管してある場所という意味の語である。

Let's Try

Part 5 短文穴埋め問題 ···

1. Dr. Harris, _____ book was just published last week, will be the main speaker of the coming annual conference.

   (A) who

   (B) that

   (C) whom

   (D) whose

2. The merger, _____ will be announced next week, must be a considerable shock to the IT business.

   (A) which

   (B) whose

   (C) who

   (D) when

3. _____ customers say about our products and service carries weight in order to keep our business going.

   (A) Which

   (B) Who

   (C) What

   (D) Of which

4. Those _____ complete the special training can be a candidate for the post.

   (A) whom

   (B) who

   (C) which

   (D) whose

5. They officially announced the standards _____ the government measures the changes in the environment.

   (A) what

   (B) which

   (C) by which

   (D) that

Questions 1-4 refer to the following letter.

Ms. Elizabeth Jones
Precision Pipes Trading Inc.
394 St. Paul Avenue
Cincinnati, Ohio

Dear Ms. Jones,
We are pleased that you have chosen our company to be your ------- distributor in France,
and we are confident that you have made the right choice. We have prepared all the required
documents for export from the United States to an EU country. ------- the first order of 80
large pipes for the construction of an oil pipeline, we expect it ------- at the port of Calais in
two weeks' time. We will send three trucks, as requested, which will take the pipes to our
warehouse 20 km from the port. -------.

Kind regards,
John Trent

1. (A) singular
   (B) sole
   (C) personal
   (D) unique

2. (A) With regards to
   (B) Despite
   (C) Being concerned about
   (D) At the same time as

3. (A) would arrive
   (B) arriving
   (C) to arrive
   (D) arrive

4. (A) From there, a ship will carry them to
       the customer.
   (B) After that, we will wait for the
       documents to be arranged.
   (C) Our workers will then load all the
       pipes onto the trucks.
   (D) We will then transport them to their
       final destination.

読解編 ····〔Double Passages 1〕

例題

Madison Valley Community Center Volunteer Program

Requirements ◀─────────────────────────────── 【Requirements】 Q1

Proof of age (minimum 18 years)

Recommendation from current or former employer

Completed application forms

Commitment to three months' full-time volunteer work

Generally neat appearance

Positive attitude

Responsibilities ◀────────────────────────── 【Responsibilities】 Q2

The successful candidate will work at the Ely Community Center with children and adults who have mental and physical disabilities. Duties include interacting with the children in the playroom in the morning and taking the adults outside in the afternoon. There are also opportunities to teach reading and writing skills. The hours will be from 10:00 to 4:30 five days a week and one Saturday morning each month. This job would be especially suitable for university graduates.

Living Arrangements ◀─────────────────────── 【Arrangements】 Q3

The volunteers will live together in a house not far from the community center. Bus fares will be paid in full and free meals will be provided at the center. The volunteers will also receive a small living allowance.

The deadline for applications is May 12.

Please send an email and attach your resume to Christine O'Neill at Chris@elycenter.

To: Christine O'Neill

From: Jeff Berry

Date: May 13

Re: Volunteering

Attachments: Application, letter of recommendation

Dear Ms. O'Neill

I saw your request for volunteers on the bulletin board at Swansea library, and am

55

sending my application together with my resume and letter of recommendation. I have been active in volunteer work throughout my time at high school, and now that I have finished my university degree, I would like to return to volunteer work for a short while before I pursue my career.

I apologize for sending this application after the due date. To tell the truth, I saw the notice for the first time last night as I returned books to the library, and I have sent this email more or less immediately. I hope that you will overlook the deadline and consider my application.

Thank you for your time,

Sincerely,
Jeff Berry

Q1. What is NOT required to work as a volunteer?

  (A) An optimistic personality
  (B) Official documents
  (C) fashionable clothes
  (D) Twelve weeks' free time

Q2. What do the volunteer's duties include?

  (A) Looking after some adults
  (B) Teaching people to speak
  (C) Writing reports
  (D) Playing with children after lunch

Q3. What arrangements will be made for the volunteers?

  (A) They will receive a train pass.
  (B) They will be given accommodation.
  (C) They can stay at the community center.
  (D) They will be paid a full wage.

Q4. Where did Jeff see this notice?

  (A) In a magazine
  (B) On the Internet
  (C) Around the university
  (D) At the library

Q5. What might make it difficult for Jeff to become a volunteer?

  (A) He missed the application deadline.
  (B) He is no longer a university student.
  (C) He doesn't have a reference.
  (D) He wrote a letter instead of an email.

ここがポイント！　設問に目を通しながら、キーワードの類義語、関連語を本文中に探そう。

　TOEIC の Part 7 の問題をできるだけ効率よく解くためには、質問の答えが本文のどの部分に書かれているかを素早くつかむことが大切です。TOEIC では、類義語や反意語を使った言い換えが多く用いられます。Part 7 では、設問と本文の中で異なる表現を用い、ほぼ同じことを表すということが頻繁に行われます。設問と本文に交互に目を通しながら、設問のキーワードとなる語の関連語を本文中に探し、答えがどこに書かれているかを絞り込む習慣をつけましょう。

　上の例題では、Q1 の required と本文の Requirements、Q2 の duties と本文の Responsibilities が関連し、Q3 は設問と本文で同じ arrangements が使われていますので、該当部分をもう少し詳しく読むと、たいていの場合、設問の答えが見つけられます。Q1 は「ボランティアに要求されていないもの」ですから、Requirements に含まれていないものですが、(A) は 6 点目の positive attitude、(B) は 1 〜 3 点目、(D) は 4 点目「3 か月間常勤でボランティアを行うこと」と言い換えられますので、(C)「おしゃれな服装」が正解です。同様に、Q2 は「ボランティアの義務に含まれるもの」ですから、Responsibilities に含まれているもの、Q3 は「ボランティアのために手配されていること」ですから Living Arrangements の詳細を読みましょう。

例題の正解

Q1 (C)　Q2 (A)　Q3 (B)　Q4 (D)　Q5 (A)

最重要ヴォキャブラリー　◀ 27　◀ 28

☐ **appearance** [əpíərəns] 名「外見」「登場」　make an appearance で動詞の appear [əpíər]「登場する」とほぼ同意。

☐ **arrangement** [əréindʒmənt] 名「手配」「取り決め」「整理」　make arrangements は「手配する」、special arrangements は「特別な手配」、make alternative arrangements は「予定のものとは別の手配をする」という意味の表現。動詞は arrange [əréindʒ]「手配する」「取り決める」。

☐ **attach** [ətǽtʃ] 動「添付する」「配属される」　名詞は attachment [ətǽtʃmənt]「愛着」「付属品」「(e メールの) 添付ファイル」「添付書類」で、TOEIC では「(e メールの) 添付ファイル」の意味で使われることが最も多い。

☐ **attitude** [ǽtitjùːd] 名「態度」「姿勢」　attitude to [toward, about] で「〜に対する態度」という意味。

☐ **availability** [əvèiləbíləti] 名「入手可能性」「利用できること」「有効性」　形容詞の available [əvéiləbl]「入手できる」「役に立つ」「利用できる」「(人が) 都合がつく」同様、多義語で状況によって訳し分ける必要がある。

☐ **facility** [fəsíləti] 名「施設」「設備」「才能」　TOEIC では、「施設」「設備」の意味で使われることがほとんどである。また、宿泊施設の部屋の説明などで private facilities と言うと、浴室とトイレを指す。

☐ **former** [fɔ́ːrmər] 形「以前の」「もとの」　同意語に ex がある。

☐ **furnish** [fɔ́ːrniʃ] 動「(家や部屋に) 家具を備え付ける」「提供する」　日本ではあまり一般的ではないが、欧米では、Furnished House [Room]「家具つき貸家 [部屋]」は賃貸広告に頻出の表現である。

☐ **graduate** [grǽdʒuət] 名「卒業生」/ [grǽdʒuèit] 動「卒業する」　graduate from 〜で「〜を卒業する」という意味。名詞と動詞で発音が異なるので注意。

☐ **interact** [ìntərǽkt] 動「相互に作用する」「交流する」　interact with 〜「〜と相互作用する」「〜と交流する」のように用いる。名詞は interaction [ìntərǽkʃən]「交流」「相互作用」。

☐ **occupant** [ákjupənt] 名「入居者」「(乗り物に) 乗っている人」　「入居者」は resident [rézədənt]、「(乗り物に) 乗っている人」は passenger [pǽsəndʒər] に言い換え可能である。

☐ **optimistic** [àptəmístik] 形「楽観的な」「のんきな」　反意語は、pessimistic [pèsəmístik]「悲観的な」。名詞は optimism [áptəmìzm]「楽観主義」「のんきな性格」と optimist [áptəmist]「楽天主義者」。

- ☐ **overlook** [òuvərlúk] 動「見落とす」「大目に見る」「見渡す」 「見落とす」の意味では、同意語に miss [mís] がある。「大目に見る」の意味では、overlook errors、overlook one's mistake のように用い、寛大な気持ちで失敗を許す場合に用いる。

- ☐ **positive** [pázətiv] 形「確信している」「前向きな」「肯定的な」 「確信している」の同意語に certain [sə́ːrtn] や sure [ʃúər]、「前向きな」の同意語に optimistic [àptəmístik] がある。「前向きな」「肯定的な」の反意語は negative [négətiv]「後ろ向きな」「否定的な」。

- ☐ **proof** [prúːf] 名「証拠」「校正刷り」 動「(ページなどを) 校正する」 動詞の意味の場合、proofread [prúːfrìːd] を用いるほうが一般的。

- ☐ **pursue** [pərsúː] 動「続ける」「追及する」「追跡する」 「続ける」の意味では、pursue a career「キャリアを積む」のように、活動や計画の続行に用いる。名詞は pursuit [pərsúːt]「追及」「追跡」「娯楽」。

- ☐ **recommendation** [rèkəmendéiʃən] 名「推薦」「推薦状」 「推薦状」の意味では、letter of recommendation や reference [réfərəns] と言い換えられることが多い。

- ☐ **reference** [réfərəns] 名「言及」「参照」「身元照会」「(雇い主に出す) 紹介状」 TOEIC では、「(雇い主に出す) 紹介状」の意味で使われることが最も多く、この場合、letter of reference と言われることもある。

- ☐ **refurbish** [rifə́ːrbiʃ] 動「改装する」「一新する」 名詞は refurbishment [rifə́ːrbiʃmənt]「改装」「新装」。

- ☐ **renovate** [rénəvèit] 動「刷新する」「修復する」 名詞は renovation [renəvéiʃən]「刷新」「修復」で、renovation work は「修復作業」、under renovation は「修復中で」という意味。

- ☐ **spacious** [spéiʃəs] 形「広々とした」 関連語に、wide [wáid]「幅が広い」、large [láːrdʒ]「大きい」、roomy [rúːmi]「広々とした」がある。

- ☐ **suitable** [súːtəbl] 形「適した」「ふさわしい」 反意語は unsuitable [ʌ̀nsúːtəbl]「不適当な」。「ふさわしい人 [もの]」という場合は、right person [thing] と言うほうが一般的である。

Let's Try

Part 7 読解問題 ···

Questions 1-5 refer to the following advertisement and email.

Apartment for Rent

Address: Euclid Ave, 39284 New York, United States
Availability: From Mar. 10
Property type: Apartment

DESCRIPTION
Featuring a private patio and a spacious kitchen, this newly renovated first-floor apartment in the Bronx is just a five-minute walk from the Harlem Bridge and the Upper Manhattan area.

The modern apartment is located within a townhouse building, and features a large living area with double bed and flat-screen TV. The apartment is fully furnished. Car parking is not available.

Located two blocks away, the subway station provides direct links to Times Square and Grand Central Station, which are a short 20 minutes away. The Yankee Sports Stadium and the Bronx Arts Museum are within a 10-minute walk of the apartment.

The surrounding area offers plenty of restaurants and bars, and there are several supermarkets and malls nearby.

HOUSE RULES for OCCUPANTS
Deposit +1 month's rent in advance
Smoking, pets, and children prohibited

Contact Kim Lee 385 5293
Email: Lee29@quickmail.com

To: Kim Lee
From: Helen Clayton

Dear Mr. Lee,
I saw your advertisement for an apartment to rent listed in the online magazine Smartrent. The photos looked great, and I would very much like to view the apartment. I arrived in New York last week and am currently staying in a hotel, so would like to find a place as soon as I can. I noticed that the apartment will be available to rent from Tuesday. Would it be possible to view it tomorrow evening, i.e., Monday? I am afraid I am working during the day so could not come over before seven o'clock. Also, could you tell me if the apartment building has a secure place where I could keep a bicycle?

Looking forward to hearing from you,
Helen Clayton

---

1. What is a feature of the apartment to rent?
   (A) It has been refurbished.
   (B) It is next to Grand Central Station.
   (C) It contains two beds.
   (D) It is partly furnished.

2. Who would be most likely to rent this apartment?
   (A) A single person with a cat
   (B) A couple with no children
   (C) A small family
   (D) A business person with a car

3. What date is it today?
   (A) March 8
   (B) March 9
   (C) March 10
   (D) March 11

4. What do we learn about Helen Clayton?
   (A) She is staying at a friend's apartment.
   (B) She is a native of New York City.
   (C) She has an evening job.
   (D) She wants to see the apartment soon.

5. What does Helen Clayton want to know?
   (A) If she can keep a pet
   (B) If Kim is free on Tuesday
   (C) If the apartment has a parking facility for a bicycle
   (D) If she can visit at 7 a.m.

Unit 8

文法編 ……〔比較〕

例題

Kelly's carries _____ expensive merchandise than the other stores in the town.

 (A) most   (B) much   (C) more   (D) mostly

ここがポイント！ 物事を比較して、「同じくらい」「こちらのほうが〜」「一番〜」

 Unit 1 で学習したように、形容詞や副詞は、物事の性質や状態、程度を表現します。形容詞や副詞には、「原級」と呼ばれる元の形以外に「比較級」と「最上級」という形があり、2つの物事を比較して「AとBが同じくらい〜」という場合に原級、「AのほうがBより、より〜だ」という場合に比較級、すべての中で「最も〜である」という場合に最上級を用います。まず、原級から比較級、最上級への変化のルールを理解し、どの形を使うべき状況なのかを見極めましょう。

 上の問題では、than 〜「〜より」という語があるので、Kelly's と the other stores「他の店」の商品価格の2つを比較して、Kelly's のほうが高いと言っています。expensive「高価な」は、more expensive、most expensive と変化する形容詞ですから、空欄には (C) more が適当ということになります。

正解 (C)

問題文の訳：ケリーズは、町の他の店よりもっと高価な商品を扱っている。

 比較表現に関する基本と応用事項をまとめます。

〈形容詞、副詞の変化の3つのルール〉

ルール1 比較級は原級の語尾に -er、最上級は -est を付ける。（1音節の語と2音節の語の一部）
 例：cheap – cheaper - cheapest

ルール2 比較級は原級の前に more、最上級は most を付ける。（2音節の語の大部分と3音節以上の語）
 例：successful – more successful – most successful

ルール3 不規則な活用をするもの
 例：many / much – more – most   good / well – better – best
   bad / ill – worse – worst   little – less – least
   late – latter[later] – last[latest] far – farther[further] – farthest[furthest]

〈基本となる比較表現〉

原級表現 A +動詞+ as 原級 as + B 「AはBと同じくらい〜」
 This model is **as** profitable **as** the previous one.
 A +否定文+ as 原級 as + B 「AはBほど〜ではない」
 This model is not **as** profitable **as** the previous one.

比較級表現 A +動詞+比較級 (than B)「AはBより、より〜」
 This model is more profitable **than** the previous one.

最上級表現 A +動詞+ the 最上級 + of[in] B「AはBの中で最も〜」
 This model is **the** most profitable **of** all.

〈比較に関する慣用表現〉

[比較級の強調] much, even, far, still「ずっと」

The construction finished **much** earlier than we had expected.

[最上級の強調] by far「群を抜いて」

Ms. Lee is **by far** the most creative and innovative engineer of all.

[倍数表現] ... times as ～ as「…倍～だ」（倍数表現）「2倍」の場合は、twice as ～ as

This year, we received three **times as** many applications **as** last year.

[比較級 and 比較級] 「ますます～だ」

More and more retailers are resorting to part-time employees in their business.

[the＋比較級 , the＋比較級] 「～すればするほど…だ」

The more people there are, **the more difficult** it is to reach a conclusion.

最重要ヴォキャブラリー 🔊 29 🔊 30

☐ **affordable** [əfɔ́ːrdəbl] 形「**手頃な価格の**」「**安価な**」 類義語に、reasonable [ríːzənəbl]「手頃な」「妥当な」、cheap [tʃíːp]「安い」、inexpensive [inikspénsiv]「（値段が）高くない」がある。

☐ **dependable** [dipéndəbl] 形「**頼りになる**」「**信頼できる**」 同意語に reliable [riláiəbl] がある。動詞の depend [dipénd] を用いた It/That depends.「状況次第だ」という表現も TOEIC に頻出。

☐ **enhance** [inhǽns] 動「**高める**」「**増す**」 通例、能力や技術などに使う。

☐ **exchange** [ikstʃéindʒ] 名「**交換**」「**為替**」「**交流**」 TOEIC では、exchange rate「為替レート」、exchange market「為替市場」、foreign exchange「外国為替」、stock exchange「株式取引所」などの表現が頻出。

☐ **excursion** [ikskə́ːrʒən] 名「**遠足**」「**小旅行**」 make [go on] an excursion は「遠足に行く」という意味。TOEIC では、trip [tríp] や journey [dʒə́ːrni]「旅行」と言い換えられることもある。

☐ **furniture** [fə́ːrnitʃər] 名「**家具**」 不可算名詞で、複数形にならないことに注意。TOEIC では、desk や chair といった具体的な家具名と言い換えられることも多い。

☐ **merchandise** [mə́ːrtʃəndàiz] 名「**商品**」 動「**取引をする**」 名詞の場合、不可算名詞で複数形にはならないことに注意。数える場合は a piece of merchandise や two pieces of merchandise のように言う。同意語に goods [gúdz] がある。

☐ **post** [póust] 動「**掲示する**」「**郵送する**」「**計上する**」 ビジネスでは、post a gain「収益 [損失] を計上する」や post sales「売り上げを計上する」といった表現に用いられることが多い。

☐ **present** [préznt] 形「**出席している**」「**現在の**」 「出席している」の意味の反意語は absent [ǽbsənt]「欠席している」。「現在の」の意味の関連語に、past [pǽst]「過去の」や future [fjúːtʃər]「未来の」がある。

☐ **resort** [rizɔ́ːrt] 動「**（手段に）頼る**」「**（方法に）訴える**」 resort to violence [force]「暴力 [武力] に訴える」のように、好ましくない方法をやむなく使用する場合に用いられることが多い。

☐ **saving** [séiviŋ] 名「**節約**」（複数形で）「**貯蓄**」 make huge savings と言うと「大いに節約する」という意味。

☐ **slash** [slǽʃ] 動「**ざっくり切る**」「**大幅に削減する**」 名「**さっと切りつけること**」「**切り傷**」「**大幅削減**」 「大幅に削減する」「大幅削減」の意味では、同意語に cut がある。

Let's Try

Part 5 短文穴埋め問題 ··

1. We are looking for an office which is _____than the present one and still affordable.

(A) space

(B) spacious

(C) more spacious

(D) the most spacious

2. The new instruction manuals are not _____as the old ones.

(A) as complicated

(B) more complicated

(C) complicated than

(D) most complicated

3. Because the exchange rate dramatically fell, we will post _____ loss in the history of the company this year.

(A) a large

(B) the larger

(C) largest

(D) the largest

4. According to the survey results, young people have _____ interest in purchasing and exchanging goods on the Internet.

(A) the more

(B) many

(C) more than

(D) more and more

5. The longer the current recession lasts, the _____ we will end up in a merger.

(A) likely

(B) more likely

(C) most likely

(D) likeliest

Questions 1-4 refer to the following email advertisement.

Great Outdoors
Stock Clearance: Summer Warehouse Sale Now On!

All stock must GO! Our big clearout gives you the chance to make HUGE savings on hundreds of great outdoor products. ------. Our warehouse sale is now live with at least 25% off all items. Stock is selling fast so don't wait!

Are you hoping to ------ your family tent for the summer vacation, or do you need a waterproof jacket for sudden downpours? Buy now online or in-store.

Prices ------ slashed across all departments, so whatever your next adventure, you can get outdoors for less.

Browse amazing deals and discounts on complete camping setups including tents, sleeping bags, and furniture. For little adventurers, shop in our Kids' department for dependable waterproof jackets and children's outdoor footwear, ideal for outdoor play and the ------ to school. Don't miss these great savings on outdoor gear in this, our biggest ever warehouse sale.

---

1. (A) Get great bargains at the largest sale in our 20-year history.
   (B) It's our biggest sale this year, so hurry while stocks last!
   (C) Discounts can be found on selected products for outdoor use.
   (D) Winter is coming soon, so stock up on warm clothes.

2. (A) improve
   (B) enhance
   (C) upgrade
   (D) exchange

3. (A) will be
   (B) had been
   (C) will have been
   (D) have been

4. (A) expedition
   (B) trip
   (C) excursion
   (D) voyage

読解編 ‥‥〔Double Passages 2〕

例題

Tokyo Subway Networks to Get Free Wi-fi

When you're traveling on the Tokyo subway it is difficult to get free wi-fi. For residents of Japan, this is not a great problem because commuters can check emails on their smartphones using the Wi-Fi that they have paid for through their service provider. For visitors from other countries, it is not so easy—they have to wait until their journey is finished and they can go to one of the coffee shops that offer free Wi-Fi. Well, the future will be different. The government has decided to accommodate the large numbers of visitors who will come to Japan during the Tokyo Olympics by creating free networks on many of the subway stations. This will bring Tokyo in line with many of the other world capitals. The system may also be rolled out to Osaka and other major cities.

A Tokyo-wide study will analyze the train network to reveal the most-used lines before installing the wireless systems. Any commuter is eligible to use the system. Although the wireless networks will not bring direct revenue to the train companies, it is anticipated that they will benefit because the subway system will become more attractive.

One issue with using free networks is security. The train companies recommend that anyone who wants to use this network should make sure their phone or tablet PC is secure by downloading the latest anti-virus software.

【For visitors … free Wi-Fi.】Q1

【The government … stations.】Q2

【A Tokyo-wide study … systems.】Q3

【One issue … security.】Q4

Start date for full coverage	Coverage	Usage time	Operator	No. of hotspots
December 1	143 Tokyo subway stations	3 hrs/session (no limit to number of sessions)	KM Broadband Platform Inc.	9,000

Q5

Q1. According to the article, how can **a visitor to Japan** check email?

    (A) On the subway

    (B) In a cafe

    (C) At the hotel

    (D) At a service provider's branch

Q2. Why is **the government** providing free Wi-Fi?

    (A) It wants to modernize Tokyo.

    (B) It wants to provide better service to visitors.

    (C) It will help the Olympic athletes.

    (D) To bring Tokyo in line with Osaka.

Q3. What will the government do **before installing the system**?

    (A) Determine which train lines are busiest

    (B) Consider how to collect revenue

    (C) Renovate the subway stations

    (D) Try it out in selected areas of Tokyo

Q4. What **problem** is anticipated?

    (A) Limited coverage

    (B) Lack of software

    (C) Attacks by viruses

    (D) Too many downloads

Q5. **How many sessions** can users have on the free Wi-Fi?

    (A) 3

    (B) 143

    (C) 9,000

    (D) Unlimited

（ここがポイント！）　設問の答えは、問題文に設問の順番通りに書かれている。

　問題の本文と表の中に付けられた Q1 や Q2 などのメモを見てください。それぞれの設問の答えとなる情報が書かれている箇所に付けられた印ですが、Q1 から Q5 まできれいに順番通りに並んでいます。これでわかるように、TOEIC の Part 7 では、設問の答えはほぼ設問の順番どおりに本文に書かれています。ですから、設問と本文に交互に目を通しながら、必要な部分を順番に読み進めればよいのです。すでに読んだ部分に戻る必要はほとんどありません。この際、Unit7 で取り上げたように、設問と本文中の関連語をヒントに、読むべき部分を素早く絞りこむことを忘れないようにしましょう。

　上の例題では、Q1 の a visitor to Japan と本文の visitors from other countries、Q2 と本文の the government、Q3 と本文の before installing the system、Q4 の problem と本文の issue、Q5 の How many sessions と表中の sessions が、絞り込みのヒントです。

（例題の正解）

Q1 (B)　Q2 (B)　Q3 (A)　Q4 (C)　Q5 (D)

（最重要ヴォキャブラリー）　🔊⟨31⟩ 🔊⟨32⟩

☐ **ample** [ǽmpl] 形「（あり余るほど）十分な」「広い」　「（あり余るほど）十分な」の意味の関連語に、adequate [ǽdikwət]「適当な」、enough [inʌ́f]「（必要なだけ）十分な」、sufficient [səfíʃənt]「十分な」がある。

☐ **concerning** [kənsə́:rniŋ] 前「～に関して」「～について」　フォーマルな表現である。同意語に、regarding [rigá:rdiŋ] や about がある。

☐ **coverage** [kʌ́vəridʒ] 名「報道」「補償（範囲）」「サービス区域」　TV coverage of the election と言えば、「選挙のテレビ報道」ということ。

☐ **invitation** [ìnvətéiʃən] 名「招待」「招待状」「依頼」　accept an invitation は「招待［依頼］に応じる」、decline [turn down] an invitation は「招待［依頼］を断る」という意味。

☐ **modernize** [mádərnàiz] 動「近代化する」「現代的にする」　modernise という綴りもある。名詞は modernization [màdərnaizéiʃən]「近代化」、形容詞は modern [mádərn]「現代の」「近代の」「最新式の」。

☐ **preference** [préfərəns] 名「好み」「希望」　give preference to ～は、「～を優先する」という意味。動詞は prefer [prifə́:r]「～のほうを好む」、形容詞は preferable [préfərəbl]「より望ましい」、副詞は preferably [préfərəbli]「できれば」。

☐ **reassure** [rì:əʃúər] 動「安心させる」　reassure +（人）+ that ～で「（人）に～と言って安心させる」という意味の表現。

☐ **recipient** [risípiənt] 名「受取人」「受賞者」　フォーマルな表現。類義語に receiver [risí:vər]「受取人」がある。アクセントの位置にも気をつけたい。

☐ **reveal** [riví:l] 動「明らかにする」「（隠れていたものを）見せる」　類義語に disclose [disklóuz]「（情報や身元を）公表する」がある。

☐ **venue** [vénju:] 名「会場」「開催地」　単独で用いられる他、conference venue「会議の会場」という表現が TOEIC では頻出である。

Let's Try

Part 7　読解問題 ···

Questions 1-5 refer to the following memorandum and email.

MEMORANDUM

To: All staff
Re: Year-end party
From: Caroline Davenport
Date: December 10

Yes, it's that time of year again! Dust off your party clothes and join us at the staff party, which will take place on the 20th, the last day of work for this year. We will be holding the party at the Great Lake Country Club, which is the same place we used for the Halloween party, and we have reserved the club from 7:00 pm to 11:00 pm. I'd like you to email me by December 15 to confirm whether or not you can attend. Also, please let me know if you have any special requests regarding food. I know more than a few of you are vegetarians, so I'd like to put in your requests to the hotel cooking staff as soon as possible. I'd like to reassure you that their vegetarian dishes are excellent! Finally, let me know if you want to bring a friend or partner. As always,

---

everyone gets a "plus one" for this party.

Concerning transportation, we can take you all to the venue in the company bus, which will also take you to the train station once the party finishes. If you would prefer to drive (only those who do not intend to drink!), then there is ample parking at the country club.

Looking forward to receiving your emails.

Caroline Davenport

To: Caroline Davenport

Re: Year-end party

From: Patricia Evans

Date: December 12

Dear Caroline,

Thank you for organizing the annual party. This is to let you know that I will be attending. Since last year I have become a vegan (a strict kind of vegetarian), so could you please pass on that information to the hotel staff? Also, you don't need to reserve a seat on the bus for me. As you know, I don't drink, so will be driving my car to the venue. As for the "plus one," of course I will be bringing my husband John, as always. He sends his regards.

Looking forward to it!

Catch you at work tomorrow,

Pat

---

1. What is Caroline organizing?
   (A) A lake excursion
   (B) A Halloween celebration
   (C) A year-end party
   (D) A nightclub event

2. What does Caroline want to know?
   (A) Recipients' diet preferences
   (B) How to get to the venue
   (C) If people will bring a colleague
   (D) Whether they want to cancel

3. How will most people leave the event?
   (A) By car
   (B) By bus
   (C) By train
   (D) On foot

4. What does Patricia ask Caroline to do?
   (A) Provide special food
   (B) Reserve a seat on the bus
   (C) Give her a ride
   (D) Pass on a message

5. Which of the following is probably true about Caroline?
   (A) She is a vegetarian.
   (B) She knows Patricia's husband.
   (C) She will be driving to the event.
   (D) She will accept Patricia's invitation.

Unit 9

Unit 1
Unit 2
Unit 3
Unit 4
Unit 5
Unit 6
Unit 7
Unit 8
Unit 9
Unit 10
Unit 11
Unit 12

文法編 ……〔注意すべき副詞〕

例題

Staff members _____ ready to explain the office procedures to new employees.

- (A) should always be
- (B) being always should
- (C) always be should
- (D) always should being

ここがポイント！　〈頻度〉を表す副詞（句）の位置など、副詞の細かい使い分けに注意！

　Unit1 で学習したように、副詞には、動詞、形容詞、副詞などさまざまな語句を修飾し、物事の状態をより詳しく説明する働きがあります。その中の1つに〈頻度〉を表す副詞（句）があり、文中のどの位置に用いるべきかを問う問題は、TOEIC には頻出です。他にも、注意が必要な副詞の働きを問う頻出問題がありますので、この Unit で確認しましょう。

　〈頻度〉を表す副詞（句）は、twice a week「週に2回」のように、使う人によって幅がない確定的なものと、often「しばしば」、sometimes「時々」のように、使う人によって幅のある不確定なものとに分けられます。また、一緒に使われる動詞が、一般動詞なのか、be 動詞なのか、または助動詞が用いられているのかによっても、〈頻度〉を表す副詞（句）の文中での位置は異なります。

　上の問題では、always「いつも」という頻度を表す副詞が、should「～すべき」という助動詞とともに使われています。これは、助動詞の直後に使うべきですので、(A) should always be が空欄には適当ということになります。(B) と (D) は being が使われていますが、助動詞と一緒に用いる動詞は原形でなければいけませんので、これらは正解の可能性がある選択肢ではないと判断できます。

正解　(A)

問題文の訳：スタッフは、新入社員に対して、常にオフィス内の手順を説明する用意をしておくべきだ。

1. 〈頻度〉を表す副詞の位置に関する基本的なルールをまとめます。

パターン1　文、または節の最初か最後にくるもの

　例：every day[week、month、year]、daily、monthly、quarterly、annually、once[twice] a day[week、month、year] など

Every morning the manager gives a short speech to the department staff.

The manager gives a short speech to the department staff every morning.

パターン2　be 動詞の後ろ、一般動詞の前にくるもの

　例：always、usually、frequently、often、sometimes、rarely、seldom、never など

He is usually very punctual.

He usually submits papers by a deadline.

パターン3　助動詞（完了形の中の have、has、had など助動詞扱いの語を含む）が使われている場合、助動詞の後ろにくるもの

　例：always、usually、frequently、often、sometimes、rarely、seldom、never など

He has never been late for meetings.

2. TOEIC に頻出の意味が似ている副詞の使い分けについてまとめます。

still still は「いまだに」という意味。通常、be 動詞や助動詞（助動詞扱いの語を含む）の後、一般動詞の前に置く。否定文の中では、否定語の直前に置く。

We still **have** plenty of file folders in the supply cabinet.

We have still **not** ordered file folders.

yet yet は「まだ〜ない」（否定文）、「もうすでに」（疑問文）という意味。文の最後に置く。

Have you called in a repairperson yet?

I have**n't** called in a repairperson yet.

already already は「もうすでに」という意味。平叙文で使われることが多く、通常、be 動詞や助動詞（助動詞扱いの語を含む）の後、一般動詞の前に置く。

I **have** already called in a repairperson.

I already **called** in a repairperson.

最重要ヴォキャブラリー　🔊 33 🔊 34

☐ **alert** [ələ́ːrt] 形「油断のない」動「警戒させる」名「警報」 stay alert と言うと「気を緩めずにいる」という意味。

☐ **apprehend** [æprihénd] 動「逮捕する」 同意語に arrest [ərést] があり、こちらの方が一般的な語。

☐ **cautious** [kɔ́ːʃəs] 形「慎重な」「用心深い」 「〜に注意する」と言う場合、be cautious about [of/with] 〜を用いる。名詞は caution [kɔ́ːʃən]「注意」で、use[exercise] caution で「用心する」という表現。

☐ **envelope** [énvəlòup] 名「封筒」 最初にアクセントがあることに注意しよう。

☐ **file** [fáil] 動「(申請書などを) 提出する」「整理して保管する」名「ファイル」 file a claim は「請求権を申し立てる」、file a suit は「訴訟を起こす」、file for a bankruptcy は「破産を申請する」という意味。

☐ **inter-departmental** [ìntəːrdipὰːrtméntl] 形「各部 [省 / 局] 間の」 inter- [ìntər-] が、「〜の間」という意味の接頭語であることを覚えておこう。

☐ **precautious** [prikɔ́ːʃəs] 形「用心深い」「慎重な」 名詞は precaution [prikɔ́ːʃən]「予防措置」「警戒」で、as a precaution と言うと「念のために」という意味になる。

☐ **premise** [prémis] 名「建物」「敷地」 通常、複数形で用い、on the premises と言うと「店内で」「構内で」という意味。

☐ **proper** [prápə] 形「適切な」 同意語に appropriate [əpróupriət]、suitable [súːtəbl]、right などがある。

☐ **punctual** [pʌ́ŋktʃuəl] 形「時間を守る」「期限どおりの」 同意語に on time、反意語に late [léit]「遅れた」がある。副詞は、punctually [pʌ́ŋktʃuəli]「時間通りに」。

☐ **rarely** [réərli] 副「めったに〜ない」 反意語には、frequently [fríːkwəntli]、often [ɔ́ːfən]「しばしば」がある。

☐ **repairperson** [ripéərpə̀ːrsn] 名「修理人」 同じ意味で repairman [ripéərmæ̀n] という表現もある。

☐ **seldom** [séldəm] 副「めったに〜ない」 同意語に rarely [réərli] があるが、seldom のほうがフォーマルな表現。頻度を表す副詞なので、文中で使われている動詞の種類によって、位置が異なることに注意しよう。（Unit 9 文法編参照）

Let's Try

Part 5 短文穴埋め問題 ··

1. Inter-departmental staff meetings are held _____ in Meeting Room A on the fifth floor.

    (A) always

    (B) sometimes

    (C) rarely

    (D) every week

2. Most entrepreneurs are required to file their taxes _____ .

    (A) rarely

    (B) usually

    (C) quarterly

    (D) never

3. There aren't any envelopes or file folders in the supply cabinet because they _____ .

    (A) never have ordered been

    (B) have been never ordered

    (C) have never been ordered

    (D) have been ordered never

4. All the plant workers have to fill out the time sheets twice _____ – in the morning when they arrive and in the evening when they leave.

    (A) daily

    (B) sometimes

    (C) frequently

    (D) once a day

5. Ms. Saito has _____ distributed the agendas for tomorrow's meeting.

    (A) soon

    (B) already

    (C) yet

    (D) still

Unit 1

Unit 2

Unit 3

Unit 4

Unit 5

Unit 6

Unit 7

Unit 8

Unit 9

Unit 10

Unit 11

Unit 12

Questions 1-4 refer to the following notice.

Beware of Pickpockets

We would like you all to be ------- that a gang of pickpockets has been operating in this
area in recent weeks and targeting visitors to this museum. We ask that you stay alert
at all times. -------. We have increased security around these premises and added more
closed-circuit TV cameras to monitor the situation. The police are making progress in
their investigations and are confident that they will catch the members of the pickpocket
gang soon. ------- you fall victim to a pickpocket, please contact a member of our
security team at once. Do not attempt to chase or physically apprehend pickpockets
as they ------- work as a group and may be dangerous. Finally, there is no need to
panic. If you take the proper precautions, you can enjoy your museum visit in safety.

---

1. (A) amused
　　(B) aware
　　(C) astounded
　　(D) anxious

2. (A) Make sure your bag is fastened
　　　　securely.
　　(B) Please visit the museum at another
　　　　time.
　　(C) There is no need to be cautious.
　　(D) We will inform the police
　　　　immediately.

3. (A) Since
　　(B) As
　　(C) If
　　(D) When

4. (A) logically
　　(B) naturally
　　(C) representatively
　　(D) typically

読解編 ⋯⋯〔Double Passages 3〕

例題

The results in the charts below show the excellent improvements achieved by our new graduate hires on their initial training courses. The left-hand column illustrates business knowledge and skills in key areas such as accounting and law on entering the company, and the right-hand column shows how these skills improved after one month of intensive training. We recommend implementing this course for all new employees in our headquarters in Houston, Texas, as well as for those in our subsidiaries in Singapore, Thailand, and Vietnam. We believe this course will be especially useful for liberal arts graduates, who may not have had so much exposure to the topics taught in the course. Naturally, attendance at this intensive course means that the graduates will not start actual work at the company until the second month, but we believe that this scheme will benefit the company greatly in the long run. Usually it takes new workers around a year before they contribute to profits. We think that this course will shorten this period by around three months.◀

【Usually it takes ... three months.】
Q4

Q5

Improvement skills for new graduates

Parcent

Before training　　After training

Q1. What is the opinion of the report regarding training results?

(A) They are terrible.
(B) They are mixed.
(C) They are outstanding.
(D) It is extremely difficult to tell.

Q2. Who received training?

(A) Company staff
(B) College students
(C) University undergraduates
(D) Experienced businesspeople

Q3. For what reason would liberal arts graduate be likely to benefit most from the training?

(A) They lived in Singapore.
(B) They probably didn't study the subjects covered in the lessons.
(C) They are staff at the head office.
(D) They probably don't like law.

Q4. How long will it take for the workers to benefit the company?

(A) One month
(B) Two months
(C) Nine months
(D) Twelve months

Q5. Which area of study improved by the largest share?

(A) Statistics
(B) Law
(C) Accounting
(D) Presentations

（ここがポイント！） 文書やグラフ・表の中のデータを使って計算する場合は、落ち着いて！

　TOEIC の Part 7 では、passage の中にある数的データを使って計算をしなければいけない問題があります。特に多いのが、グラフや表などが使われている場合です。double passages の場合、2つの文書や表などのうちの1つを見れば計算できるものと、両方にある情報を使う必要があるものがあります。

　いずれにしても、数学のテストではありませんので、計算自体は比較的シンプルなものです。しかし、限られた時間の中で多くの問題を解く必要がある TOEIC では、気持ちが焦ってしまい、もったいない間違いをしてしまいがちです。数値だけを見て答えを選ぶのではなく、文法的な知識を使って、関係する部分を落ち着いて正確に読み取ることが大切です。

　例題では、文書の最後の部分に Q4 のカギがあります。「通常新入社員が会社の利益に貢献するまでには1年くらいかかるが、このコースによって、その期間が3か月短くなると考えている」ここでは、＜差異＞を表す by を見落とさないようにすることが必須です。通常1年だが、それより3か月短縮されるということで、正解は (C)「9か月」です。Q5 では設問の by the largest share「最も大きく」を正確に読み取りましょう。伸び率が一番大きかった分野ということで、3倍になっている (B)「法律」が正解です。

（例題の正解）
Q1 (C)　Q2 (A)　Q3 (B)　Q4 (C)　Q5 (B)

最重要ヴォキャブラリー　◀ 35　◀ 36

☐ **accounting** [əkáuntiŋ] 名「会計」「会計学」「経理」　accounting department は「経理部」という意味。

☐ **adhesive** [ædhíːsiv] 名「接着剤」形「粘着性の」　adhesive tape は「接着テープ」、adhesive plaster は「ばんそうこう」のこと。

☐ **attendance** [əténdəns] 名「出席」「出席［入場］者数」　take attendance は「出席を取る」という意味。

☐ **attention** [əténʃən] 名「注意」「配慮」「(機械などの) 手入れ」　pay attention to ～は「～に注意を払う」という意味。for the attention of ～は、公的な手紙の冒頭で「～宛」という意味で用いられ、省略形は attn. である。

☐ **contribute** [kəntríbjuːt] 動「貢献する」「～の一因となる」　名詞は contribution [kὰntrəbjúːʃən]「貢献」「寄付」と contributor [kəntríbjutər]「寄付者」「出資者」。

☐ **exposure** [ikspóuʒər] 名「(危険などに) さらされること」「発覚」「体験すること」　動詞は expose [ikspóuz]「(危険などに) さらす」「暴露する」「体験させる」。

☐ **installment** [instɔ́ːlmənt] 名「分割払いの一回分」「(連載や連続番組の) 一回分」　pay in [by] monthly installments「月賦で支払う」や pay in [by] 5 installments「5回払いする」のように用いる。

☐ **intensive** [inténsiv] 形「徹底的な」「集中的な」　反意語は、extensive [iksténsiv]「幅広い」「広大な」。名詞は intensity [inténsəti]「強度」「激しさ」「熱心さ」、動詞は intensify [inténsəfài]「強化する」「(量や度数を) 増す」。

☐ **ship** [ʃíp] 動「輸送する」「船積みする」　ship + (物) + to + (場所)「(物) を (場所) に送る」のように、方向を表す表現とともに用いることが多い。

☐ **shorten** [ʃɔ́ːrtn] 動「縮める」「短くする」　反意語は、lengthen [léŋkθən]「長くする」「伸ばす」「延長する」。

☐ **undergraduate** [ʌ̀ndərgrǽdʒuət] 名「(大学の) 学部生」形「学部の」「学生の」　関連語として、graduate [grǽdʒuət]「卒業生」、postgraduate [póustgrǽdʒuət] 名「大学院生」形「大学院の」「学部卒業後の」がある。

75

Let's Try

Questions 1-5 refer to the following email and invoice.

To: Tod Schmidt
From: Virginia Tregenza
Subject: Invoice
Date: April 1

Dear Mr. Schmidt,

Please find attached our invoice for your latest order of office furniture. We would like to apologize for the delay in the delivery of the Workspace office desk and chair sets. The reason is that this item is so popular that we ran out of supplies and had to order them from our main factory in Milwaukee. Instructions for assembly are included in the boxes. Glue, screws, and bolts are also included. To complete the assembly process, all you will need is a screwdriver. We recommend that you budget at least 40 minutes for the assembly of each set. Replacement parts, such as rollers for the chair legs, are available on request. Regarding your question about maintenance, the desks do not require polishing or any other kind of attention. To clean, simply wipe with a damp cloth once a month or so.

Best regards,
Virginia Tregenza

Classy Furniture Inc. 523 Edison St. Memphis, Tennessee Phone: 3924-2738 email: info@classfurn.com	INVOICE Date: 4/2		Ship to: Tod Schmidt 91210 Beverley Avenue, Downton, Kansas Phone: 2424-5232
Salesperson	**Date shipped**	**Shipped via**	**Terms**
Virginia Tregenza	March 24	Truck	Credit card (single payment)
Description	**Quantity**	**Unit price**	**Amount**
Workspace desk and chair set	15	$200	$3,000
Table light	15	$40	$600
Desk organizer	10	$8	$80
		Subtotal	$3,680
		Sales tax	$320
		Shipping & handling	$0.00
		Total due	**$4,000**

1. Why was the delivery delayed?
   (A) An accident occurred in the factory.
   (B) It was difficult to match the chair and table numbers.
   (C) The order arrived too late.
   (D) Demand for the items was too high.

2. What is NOT included in the package?
   (A) Adhesive
   (B) Bolts
   (C) Screwdriver
   (D) Screws

3. What advice does Ms. Tregenza give?
   (A) Spend 40 minutes assembling each desk
   (B) Buy rollers for each of the chair legs
   (C) Polish the desks regularly
   (D) Attend to the items monthly

4. How will Mr. Schmidt pay for the items?
   (A) By credit card
   (B) By check
   (C) By cash
   (D) In installments

5. How much were the items in total before tax?
   (A) $4,000
   (B) $3,680
   (C) $3,000
   (D) $600

Unit 1
Unit 2
Unit 3
Unit 4
Unit 5
Unit 6
Unit 7
Unit 8
Unit 9
Unit 10
Unit 11
Unit 12

77

文法編 ……〔前置詞〕

> **例題**
>
> The report was full _____ valuable information that could be put to good use.
>
>   (A) with   (B) of   (C) by   (D) in

ここがポイント！ 前置詞は、どれだけ多くの用法を覚え、使いこなせるかが勝負

　前置詞は、後の名詞や名詞相当語句とともに、形容詞や副詞のように、物事の状態や動向についてより詳細な情報を与える働きをします。後に続く名詞、名詞相当語句の意味次第で、使うべき前置詞が決まる場合もありますし、また、前置詞が異なると、建物の中なのか、建物周辺なのか、といったような違いが出てくる場合もあり、その時には文脈から判断しなければなりません。TOEIC では、前置詞単独の働きを問う問題、前置詞を含む慣用表現、前置詞（句）と次の Unit 11 で取り上げる接続詞との使い分けが問われます。

　上の問題では、空欄の前に be full という表現がありますので、be full of ～「～でいっぱいである」という慣用表現に関する問題ではないかと予想をします。文全体の意味を考えると自然な内容になりますので、空欄には、(B) of が適当ということになります。

正解 (B)

問題文の訳：報告書は、上手に利用できそうな貴重な情報が満載だった。

　以下に、TOEIC に頻出の前置詞単独の用法を提示します。

> **頻出前置詞の基本的な用法と意味**
>
> ここに挙げるのは、基本中の基本ばかりですから、一度辞書を使って、他にどのような用法があるのかを確認しましょう。
>
> | | | |
> |---|---|---|
> | at | 〈一点〉 | 「（場所、時間ともに）～に、～で」 |
> | by | 〈位置〉 | 「そばに」 |
> | | 〈手段〉 | 「～によって」 |
> | for | 〈方向〉 | 「～に向かって」 |
> | | 〈目標〉 | 「～のために」 |
> | from | 〈起点〉 | 「（場所、時間ともに）～から」 |
> | in | 〈内部〉 | 「～の中に」 |
> | | 〈状態〉 | 「～の状況で」 |
> | of | 〈起源〉 | 「～から」 |
> | | 〈所有〉 | 「～の」 |
> | on | 〈接触〉 | 「～に接して」 |
> | to | 〈到達点〉 | 「～へ」 |
> | with | 〈同伴〉 | 「～と一緒に」 |
> | | 〈手段〉 | 「～を使って」 |

以下に、TOEIC によく出題される、混同しやすい前置詞の用法を紹介します。

〔時〕に関係する前置詞

at: 後には、〈時刻〉、noon、night、midnight など

Lunch break starts **at** 12:30.

on: 後には、〈曜日〉〈日付〉など

A fiscal year starts **on** April 1 in Japan.

in: 後には、〈月〉〈季節〉〈年〉、the morning[afternoon、evening] など

New employees will be given a tour of the facilities **in** the afternoon.

in:〈時の経過〉「〜経ったら」

We hope to arrange a joint venture with a company in Vietnam **in** three months.

within:〈時の経過〉「〜のうちには」

I hope they will respond to our inquiry **within** a few days.

by:〈期限〉「〜までに」

We hope to sign a contract **by** January 31.

until:〈継続〉「〜までずっと」

The manager will be out of the office **until** next Wednesday.

for:〈期間〉「〜の間」 後には、ten days や a few years のように、期間の長さを表す表現。

The main office has been at the present site **for** 30 years.

during:〈期間〉「〜の間」 後には、特定の期間を表す winter holidays や lunch break などの表現。

They decided to turn off all the lights in the office **during** the lunch break.

since:〈起点〉「〜からずっと」

The main office has been at the present site **since** the foundation of the company.

〔程度〕〔差異〕を表す前置詞

by: 「〜の違いで」

Our international sales increased **by** 15%.

〔（通信や交通）手段〕を表す前置詞

by: 後には、無冠詞、単数形の表現がくる by car、by email

Most of the staff commute to the office **by** car.

on、in: 後には、冠詞や代名詞を伴った表現や複数形の名詞がくる on the plane、in her car、in letters

The quickest way to move goods overseas is **on** planes.

with: 後には、道具を表す表現がくる with a credit card

It is common for customers to pay **with** a credit card when they go abroad.

前置詞を含む慣用表現は非常に数が多く、下のリストは一部です。日常的に、前置詞と前後の語句の結びつきを意識しながら知っている表現を増やしていきましょう。

覚えておきたい前置詞を含む慣用表現

according to 〜：〜によると	account for 〜：〜を占める、〜を説明する
agree to 〜：〜に同意する	agree with 〜：〜の意見に賛成する
be accustomed to 〜：〜に慣れている	be aware of 〜：〜に気づく
be based on 〜：〜に基づいて	be dependent on 〜 / depend[rely] on 〜：〜次第である、〜に頼る
be disappointed with 〜：〜に落胆する	be eligible for 〜：〜の資格がある

be familiar with ～：～になじみがある	be inferior[superior] to ～：～より劣る［優れている］
be made of ～：～でできている	be similar to ～：～に類似している
because of ～、due to ～：～のせいで	benefit from ～：～の恩恵を受ける
compete with ～：～と競う	concentrate on ～：～に集中する
consist of ～：～で構成されている	contribute to ～：～に貢献する
deal with ～：～を処理する	in spite of ～：～にもかかわらず
instead of ～：～のかわりに	on behalf of ～：～の代わりに、～を代表して
on purpose：故意に	on time：時間通りに
pay for ～：～の支払いをする、～の分の代金を払う	prepare for ～：～の準備をする
prior to ～：～に先立って	prohibit from ～：～を禁止する
replace with ～：～と交換［交替］する	result in ～：～という結果になる
substitute for ～：～の代わりをする	succeed in ～：～に成功する
thanks to ～：～のおかげで	wait for ～：～を待つ
withdraw from ～：～から手を引く	

最重要ヴォキャブラリー　🔊 37　🔊 38

☐ **abroad** [əbrɔ́ːd] 副「**海外で**」「**外国で**」「海外［外国］へ行く」は、go [travel] abroad と言い、abroad の前に to や in などの前置詞をつけないことに気を付けよう。

☐ **accustomed** [əkʌ́stəmd] 形「**～することに慣れている**」 同意語に used [júːst] があり、be accustomed [used] to ～「～に慣れている」のように用いる。

☐ **argument** [ɑ́ːrɡjumənt] 名「**口論**」「**議論**」 動詞は argue [ɑ́ːrɡjuː]「言い争う」「議論する」。argue with ～で「～と議論する」、argue about ～で「～について議論する」という意味。

☐ **compete** [kəmpíːt] 動「**競争する**」 compete for ～は「～を求めて争う」、compete with [against] ～は「～と競合する」という意味。名詞の competition [kɑmpətíʃən]「競争」、competitor [kəmpétətər]「競争相手」「ライバル」、形容詞の competitive [kəmpétətiv]「競合する」「競争力がある」も TOEIC には頻出。

☐ **concentrate** [kɑ́nsəntrèit] 動「**集中する**」「**凝縮する**」 concentrate on ～は「～に集中する」という意味。名詞は concentration [kɑ̀nsəntréiʃən]「集中」。

☐ **convince** [kənvíns] 動「**納得させる**」「**～するように説得する**」 「～するように説得する」の意味では、persuade [pərswéid] と言い換え可能。形容詞は convinced [kənvínst]「確信した」「納得した」、名詞は conviction [kənvíkʃən]「信念」「確信」。

☐ **familiar** [fəmíljər] 形「**馴染みの**」「**熟知している**」「**親しい**」「馴染みの」の意味の反意語は、strange [stréindʒ]「見知らぬ」。名詞は familiarity [fəmìliǽrəti]「熟知」「親しさ」。

☐ **fiscal** [fískəl] 形「**財政の**」 fiscal year は「会計年度」のことで、アメリカでは 10 月 1 日から翌年の 9 月 30 日まで、イギリスでは日本と同じく 4 月 1 日から翌年の 3 月 31 日までを指す。

☐ **foundation** [faundéiʃən] 名「**基礎**」「**設立**」「**財団**」 関連語に、動詞の found [fáund]「設立する」「基づく」、名詞の founder [fáundər]「創設者」がある。動詞の found は、過去形、過去分詞形が founded となる規則動詞である。

☐ **inferior** [infíəriər] 形「**劣った**」「**劣等感を持った**」「**下位の**」名「**（地位などが）下の人**」 反意語は superior [supíəriər]。関連語に、inferiority [infìəriɔ́ːrəti] 名「劣等」「粗悪」があり、sense of inferiority、または inferiority complex と言うと「劣等感」のこと。

□ **launch** [lɔ́ːntʃ] 動「**開始する**」「**売り出す**」 「開始する」の意味では start、「売り出す」の意味では issue [íʃuː] と言い換え可能。

□ **reminder** [rimáindər] 名「**督促状**」「**思い出させるもの**」 This is just a reminder that ~「~について念のためお知らせします」という表現は、相手に催促したり、締め切りを思い出させたりするメールの書き出しによく用いられる。

□ **stiff** [stíf] 形「**硬い**」「**厳しい**」 stiff competition は「厳しい競争」という意味で、類義語に fierce [fíərs] 「熾烈な」、intense [inténs] 「激烈な」がある。

□ **superior** [supíəriər] 形「**優れた**」「**上質の**」「**上位の**」 名「**上司**」 「上司」の同意語に、boss [bɔ́ːs] や supervisor [súːpərvàizər] があり、その反意語は subordinate [səbɔ́ːrdənət] 「部下」である。関連語として、superiority [səpìəriɔ́ːrəti] 名「**卓越**」「**優位**」も覚えておこう。

□ **valuable** [vǽljuəbl] 形「**有益な**」「**高価な**」「**貴重な**」 類義語に、precious [préʃəs] 「貴重な」「高価な」や priceless [práislis] 「非常に貴重な」がある。

□ **venture** [véntʃər] 名「**冒険的事業**」 動「**(危険を冒して) 出かける**」「**思い切って言う〔行う〕**」 joint venture「ジョイントベンチャー〔合弁事業〕」や commercial〔business〕venture「ベンチャービジネス」など、カタカナ語として使われることも多い。

Let's Try

Part 5 短文穴埋め問題 ⋯⋯⋯⋯⋯⋯⋯⋯⋯⋯⋯⋯⋯⋯⋯⋯⋯⋯⋯⋯⋯⋯⋯⋯⋯⋯⋯⋯⋯⋯

1. Fifteen applications were filed _____ Monday morning for the secretary position that we announced last week.

    (A) in

    (B) on

    (C) for

    (D) at

2. The amount you will earn each month depends _____ your performance.

    (A) to

    (B) of

    (C) on

    (D) about

3. All the branch offices are equipped with sophisticated security systems which turn on automatically _____ midnight.

    (A) to

    (B) from

    (C) at

    (D) for

4. We are disappointed _____ the results of the promotion campaign we launched last month.

    (A) for

    (B) on

    (C) of

    (D) with

Unit 1 Unit 2 Unit 3 Unit 4 Unit 5 Unit 6 Unit 7 Unit 8 Unit 9 **Unit 10** Unit 11 Unit 12

5. Most of the participants arrived at the conference venue _____ their cars.

    (A) in

    (B) within

    (C) by

    (D) at

Part 6 　長文穴埋め問題 ··

Questions 1-4 refer to the following message.

Hi Barbara,

------. Peter Camden will arrive next Monday and we will pitch our new product starting
1.
from 1.00 p.m. I know you're efficient at organizing your schedule, but since we've just had
the Christmas and New Year breaks, I just wanted to make sure that you had remembered
this important event.

I'd like you and I to get together ------ the meeting with Peter in order to discuss how we
2.
will present our proposal. We have stiff competition from rival companies for this contract
so we need to present ------ argument. I've got a few ideas I'd like to show you and hear
3.
your opinion about.

How is your schedule this week? I'm free all morning tomorrow and any time after three
o'clock on Wednesday. If none of these slots work, let's talk about it ------ lunch one day
4.
before the end of the week.

All for now, George

---

1. (A) I've just heard the meeting has been
       postponed until December.
   (B) Do you have time in your schedule to
       meet Peter Camden tomorrow?
   (C) I'm sending you a reminder about the
       meeting next Monday.
   (D) I imagine you are looking forward to
       the year-end break.

2. (A) prior to
   (B) previous
   (C) after
   (D) former

3. (A) a convicted
   (B) a convincing
   (C) an absurd
   (D) an optimistic

4. (A) with
   (B) on
   (C) through
   (D) over

読解編 ·····〔Triple Passages 1〕

Accounting for Small Businesses ◄

Learn the basics of accounting for small businesses. We offer a series of 12 classes over three months. In these classes, you will learn to keep correct accounts of income and expenditure. You will also make good use of free and reasonably priced financial management software. Finally, you will study tax issues and regulations on employee pay. The teacher is a certified public accountant (CPA) with more than 20 years of experience in this field. ◄

Dates and times: Every Monday from 7:00 p.m. to 8:30 p.m. starting Sept. 1 ◄

Price: $15 per session (pay at door) or $120 for the entire course (prepaid) ◄

Place: Macclesfield College of Further Education ◄

For more details or to register, contact accountscourse@macc.ac.uk

タイトルと１文目：広告の内容

コースの期間と回数

[In these classes … employee pay.]コースの具体的な内容の説明

[The teacher is …]講師についての情報

日時

費用

場所

To: accountscourse@macc.ac.uk
From: Saul Johnson
Subject: Accounting for Small Businesses registration ◄

I'd like to register for your Accounting for Small Businesses course. I own a small but expanding landscape gardening business, and I want to be able to meet the challenges of that expansion. I would also like to know if Macclesfield College offers any other evening courses, especially those relating to business. ◄

Thank you in advance,
Saul Johnson

件名と１文目：申し込みの意志

他コースの情報提供依頼

Dear Saul,
Thank you for registering for Accounting for Small Businesses. ◄
I am sure you will find it useful. In answer to your question, yes, the college holds several courses. The ones below relate to

申し込みのお礼

Unit 1　Unit 2　Unit 3　Unit 4　Unit 5　Unit 6　Unit 7　Unit 8　Unit 9　**Unit 10**　Unit 11　Unit 12

business, but we also hold courses in music, cooking, and vehicle maintenance. ◄───────────────────

[In answer to your question …] 他コースの情報提供依頼への返答

Title	Time	Dates
Household economy	5:00 to 6:30	August 1st, 15th, 22nd, 29th
Brand awareness	5:30 to 7:00	September 5th and 15th
Improving your business website	5:30 to 7:00	September 9th, 16th, and 23rd
Presentation skills	8:00 to 9:00	October 10th and 17th

Regards,

Sally Burnett,

Manager,

Macclesfield College courses

▼

Q1. What does the advertisement offer to teach?

(A) How to record profit and loss

(B) How to start a small business

(C) How to avoid paying too much tax

(D) How to become a CPA

Q2. How much is the full course if paying at the door each time?

(A) $120

(B) $150

(C) $180

(D) $210

Q3. What can be inferred about Mr. Johnson?

(A) He does not want to take the Accounting for Small Businesses course.

(B) He wants to study accounting at a different college.

(C) He is interested in taking more than one course.

(D) He has a large garden that he enjoys landscaping.

Q4. In Mr. Johnson's email, the word "challenge" in the third line of text is closest in meaning to

(A) endeavors

(B) misunderstandings

(C) difficulties

(D) satisfaction

Q5. Which lecture title would NOT fit the categories mentioned by Sally Burnett?

(A) Improving your profile on social media

(B) Giving an effective message to an audience

(C) Accounting for daily shopping

(D) Enhancing essay-writing skills

84

ここがポイント！ やり取り形式の場合、３つの文書を行ったり来たりしながら読もう

triple passages の出題パターンの特徴に、double passages と同様に、やり取り形式になっている ものが多いことが挙げられます。組み合わせとしては、以下のようなものがあります。

- 求人広告＋求人広告への応募の添え状＋雇用主側からの返事
- 社内連絡＋それへの返事、または問い合わせ＋返事を受け取ったという確認や質問に対する返答の メール
- 商品やサービスなどの広告＋商品やサービスについての問い合わせ＋返答
- 商品やサービスなどの広告＋苦情を述べる文書＋詫び状

いずれにしても、ほとんどの場合、３つの文書の中にそれぞれ呼応している部分がありますので、そ れらに交互に目を通しながら設問に答えていくことが必要です。

例題は、自己研鑽のためのコースの広告＋参加申込みのメール＋申し込みの受領確認と追加情報とい う組み合わせです。広告では、コースの内容、講師、期間、費用、場所が述べられています。これに対 し、メールは参加申し込みの意志を示した上で、さらに関連した他のコースに関する情報提供を求めて おり、最後にコースの主催者が、受講申し込みのお礼と要望された他コースの情報を提供するというや りとりになっています。

例題の正解

Q1 (A)　Q2 (C)　Q3 (C)　Q4 (C)　Q5 (D)

最重要ヴォキャブラリー　🔊 39　🔊 40

- ☐ **audience** [ɔ́:diəns] 名「聴衆」「観客」　１つの集合体として考え、通例は単数扱いし、large[small] audience「観客が多い（少ない）」のように用いる。

- ☐ **awareness** [əwéərnis] 名「自覚」「認識」　形容詞は aware [əwéər]「認識している」で、「～を認識し ている」は be aware of ～や be aware that ～で表す。

- ☐ **certify** [sə́:rtəfài] 動「保証する」「免許状を与える」「証明する」　名詞は certification [sə̀:rtəfikéiʃən]「証 明」「認可」、certificate [sərtífikət]「証明書」「免許状」で、gift certificate と言うと「商品券」のことに なる。

- ☐ **courtesy** [kə́:rtəsi] 名「丁寧」「同意」「好意」　by courtesy of ～は「～の好意 [許可] により」とい う意味で、イラスト、写真、記事などの転載や使用許可を示す文句である。

- ☐ **endeavor** [indévər] 名「努力」「試み」動「努力する」「試みる」　名詞の類義語に effort [éfərt]、動詞 の類義語に try がある。

- ☐ **expenditure** [ikspénditʃər] 名「支出（額）」「費用」　cost や expense よりフォーマルな表現である。

- ☐ **ingredient** [ingrí:diənt] 名「材料」「要素」　「要素」の意味の類義語は element [éləmənt]。

- ☐ **legal** [lí:gəl] 形「合法的な」「法律上の」　「合法的な」の意味の反意語に illegal [ilí:gəl]、類義語に lawful [lɔ́:fəl]「適法の」がある。

- ☐ **ownership** [óunərʃìp] 名「所有」「所有権」　public/state ownership と言うと「国有」、private ownership と言うと「私有」のこと。関連語に、名詞の owner [óunər]「所有者」「飼い主」、動詞の own [óun] 「所有する」がある。

- ☐ **patent** [pǽtnt, péitnt] 名「特許（権）」形「特許を受けた」動「特許をとる」　apply for a patent で「特 許を申請する」、hold a patent は「特許権を持つ」という意味の表現。最初の部分の発音が２種類あ るので、注意しよう。

- ☐ **permission** [pərmíʃən] 名「許可」　without permission と言うと「許可なく」という意味の表現。動 詞は permit [pərmít]「許可する」「～を実現可能にする」。

Let's Try

Part 7　読解問題 ···

Questions 1-5 refer to the following recipe, email, and response.

www.deliciousrecipes.com		
Cheddar and Spring Onion Risotto with Tomatoes (feeds 4)		
Contributed by Elizabeth Crowley		
Ingredients	**Amount**	**Method**
butter	25g	STEP 1 Melt the butter in a large, shallow pan. Cook the spring onions for 4-5 minutes. Add the rice and cook, stirring, for a couple of minutes.
chopped spring onions	6	
risotto rice	150g	
white wine (optional)	A splash	STEP 2 Add the wine, and gradually stir in the stock. Heat the olive oil in a separate small pan over a medium-high heat and cook the tomatoes.
vegetable or chicken stock	750 ml	
Dijon mustard	½ tsp	
cheddar cheese, grated	100g	
olive oil	1 tbsp	STEP 3 Stir the mustard and cheese into the risotto, and season with pepper and a little salt. Spoon into warm bowls and top with the tomatoes, balsamic vinegar, and some basil.
cherry tomatoes	100g	
vinegar (use balsamic vinegar if available)	small amount	
basil, chopped	small bunch	

To:	Elizabeth Crowley
From:	Henry Higgins
Subject:	Recipe

Dear Ms. Crowley,

I have just tried out your recipe for a cheddar and spring onion risotto with tomatoes that I discovered at deliciousrecipes.com. I found it easy to make and it tasted wonderful. I run a small café in Montreal named "Cheese 'n Coffee," and would love to use this recipe as one of our signature dishes. May I have your permission to do so? I'm sure it would be a great hit with my customers.

Best regards,

Henry Higgins

To:	Henry Higgins
From:	Elizabeth Crowley
Subject:	Recipe

Dear Mr. Higgins,

I was so pleased to hear that you enjoyed the recipe I posted online. It is an old family recipe that my grandmother used to make. You are very welcome to use it in your café. I'm sure you know that there is no legal ownership of recipes and they cannot be patented, but it is nice of you to ask before you start selling the risotto. I do have one request: Could you credit me for this recipe? Please put "recipe courtesy of Elizabeth Crowley at deliciousrecipes.com" or some similar wording. I would appreciate that. Here's hoping the recipe is a great success.

Best wishes,

Elizabeth Crowley

1. According to the recipe, which item is not necessary?
 (A) Butter
 (B) Wine
 (C) Chedder cheese
 (D) Vinegar

2. What happens in the second step?
 (A) Olive oil is heated in a large pan.
 (B) Tomatoes are cooked at a high heat.
 (C) The tomatoes are chopped.
 (D) The stock is introduced.

3. What request does Henry Higgins make?
 (A) To meet the creator of the recipe
 (B) To add cheese and coffee to the recipe
 (C) To use the recipe as a key dish
 (D) To be a guest at his restaurant

4. Which word best describes Elizabeth's feeling?
 (A) Delighted
 (B) Annoyed
 (C) Neutral
 (D) Disappointed

5. What does Elizabeth ask Henry to do?
 (A) Change the recipe
 (B) Mention her name
 (C) Send another recipe
 (D) Pay her some money

Unit 1 Unit 2 Unit 3 Unit 4 Unit 5 Unit 6 Unit 7 Unit 8 Unit 9 Unit 10 Unit 11 Unit 12

Unit ⑪

例題

There has been an increase in exported and imported goods _____ the economy is strong.

  (A) because   (B) although (C) that   (D) if

ここがポイント！ 結び付ける２つの部分の「構造」と「関係」が接続詞を決める

　語と語、句と句、節と節を結び付ける働きをするのが接続詞です。これには大きく分けると２つのタイプがあります。①対等な関係にある２つの語、句、節を結び付ける等位接続詞と、②動詞の目的語を作ったり、〈理由〉や〈時〉などに関して補足的な役割をする従属接続詞です。「結び付ける２つの部分の構成が、語、句、節のどれなのか」という「構造」に関する情報と「２つの部分は、どのような意味でつながるのが自然なのか」という「関係」に関する情報を読みとることによって、用いる接続詞が決まります。

　上の問題では、空欄の前後が「製品の輸出入が増えている」「経済が好調である」とどちらも主語と述語のある節になっています。そして意味から、後半は前半部分の理由を説明していることがわかりますので、空欄以降の部分が〈理由〉を表す副詞節になるように、(A) because が空欄には適当です。

正解 (A)
問題文の訳：経済が好調なので、製品の輸出、輸入ともに増加している。

　適当な接続詞を迅速に選ぶ手がかりとなるヒントをまとめますので、覚えておきましょう。

ヒント1 頻出する接続詞の基本的な意味
　ここに挙げるのは、基本中の基本ばかりですから、一度辞書を使って、他にどのような例があるのかを確認しましょう。

代表的な例

after「〜の後に」	and「〜と…」	as「〜と同時に」	before「〜の前に」
but「しかし」	once「いったん〜すると」	or「〜または…」	since「〜以来」
so「それで〜」	until「〜まで」	when「〜のとき」	while「〜の間」

ヒント2 相関接続詞
　セットにして使う接続詞と考えてください。セット表現のうち、TOEIC ではどちらかが空欄になって出題されることがあります。
not A but B「A ではなく B」
  Our main problem is **not** the cost **but** the quality of the product.
both A and B「A も B も両方」
  They will evaluate **both** your efforts **and** performance.
not only A but also B「A だけでなく B も」
  We lost **not only** many contracts **but also** our best employees.
either A or B「A か B のどちらか」

Either he **or** I will be transferred to the new branch office.

neither A nor B「A も B も～でない」

　　　Neither he **nor** I will be transferred to the new branch office.

ヒント3　前置詞句との使い分けに注意したい接続詞

Unit10 で前置詞句を扱いましたが、後にくる表現次第で、ほぼ同じ意味の接続詞と前置詞句のどちらを使うべきかが決まります。

接続詞（後は、主語と動詞のある節）	前置詞句（後は、名詞、名詞相当語句）
<理由>　because / since「～なので」	because of / due to「～のせいで」
<逆接>　although / though /「～だけれども」 even though / while	despite / in spite of「～にもかかわらず」

Because[Since] we will move to a new office, we need to let customers know our updated contact information.

Because of[Due to] our move to a new office, we need to let customers know our updated contact information.

Although[Though, Even though, While] the hall is closed today for repairs, it will be available tomorrow.

Despite[In spite of] today's closure for repairs, the hall will be available tomorrow.

ヒント4　名詞節を導く接続詞

相関接続詞や前置詞句との使い分けに比べると、出題頻度は高くありませんが、きちんと理解しておきましょう。

　that 主語＋動詞「～であるということ」

この表現全体で名詞扱いになりますので、文の主語、目的語、補語などになります。

I think **that** some trainees will attend the meeting.

That most of the temporary staff will be laid off surprised everyone.

　if / whether 主語＋動詞「～かどうか」

意味はほぼ同じですが、〈if 主語＋動詞〉の場合は、文の主語にはなれません。

Whether[*If] our proposal will be approved or not will be announced tomorrow.

We will know **whether[if]** our proposal will be approved or not tomorrow.

最重要ヴォキャブラリー　　🔊 41　🔊 42

☐ **conflict** [kánflikt] 名「争い」「衝突」「紛争」　[kənflíkt] 動「対立する」「衝突する」　conflict of interests は「利害の衝突」、conflict of opinions は「意見の衝突」のこと。

☐ **economy** [ikánəmi] 名「経済」「倹約」　関連語として、名詞の economics [èkənámiks]「経済学」や economist [ikánəmist]「経済学者」「倹約家」、形容詞の economical [èkənámikəl]「経済的な」「つつましい」がある。

☐ **effort** [éfərt] 名「努力」　make an effort to ～「～しようと努める」は try to ～と言い換え可能。make no [little] effort to ～は「まったく［ほとんど］～しようとしない」、put effort into ～は「～に力を注ぐ」という意味の表現。

☐ **ignore** [ignɔ́ːr] 動「無視する」「見落とす」　形容詞は ignorant [ígnərənt]「無知の」「知らない」、名詞

は ignorance ［ígnərəns］「無知」「無学」「不案内」である。

- ☐ **indication** ［ìndikéiʃən］ 图「兆候」「指示」 動詞は indicate ［índikèit］「示す」「ほのめかす」、形容詞は indicative ［indíkətiv］「示す」。関連語に、名詞の indicator ［índikèitər］「指標」がある。
- ☐ **sharp** ［ʃɑ́:rp］ 副「鋭く」「(時刻を示す語の後で) ちょうど」 形「鋭い」「急激な」「痛烈な」 関連語に副詞の sharply ［ʃɑ́:rpli］「急に」「敏速に」「厳しく」がある。
- ☐ **tardy** ［tɑ́:rdi］ 形「遅ればせの」「遅刻した」 「遅刻した」の意味では同意語に late がある。
- ☐ **trainee** ［treiní:］ 图「訓練生」「研修生」 動詞の train ［tréin］ は「訓練する」という意味。-ee に「行為を受ける者」「～される人」という意味があることを覚えておくと、意味を類推しやすい。
- ☐ **update** ［ʌ̀pdéit］ 動「更新する」「最新のものにする」［ʌ́pdèit］ 图「最新情報」 形容詞は up to date ［up-to-date］「最新情報が入った」「現代的な」。

Let's Try

Part 5 短文穴埋め問題 ·····································

1. These products were neither designed _____ produced for heavy-duty industrial use.

(A) both

(B) nor

(C) so

(D) if

2. _____ in large quantities is not necessarily an indication of its quality.

(A) It is a product sold

(B) A product sells

(C) A product is sold

(D) That a product is sold

3. Those who wish to apply for this position will send their resumes _____ by fax or mail.

(A) neither

(B) both

(C) either

(D) not only

4. _____ she joined the project team late, her supervisor is confident that she will fit right in.

(A) Even though

(B) However

(C) Despite

(D) If

5. Several members indicated scheduling conflicts, _____ the meeting has been moved from Monday to Wednesday.

(A) that

(B) whether

(C) while

(D) so

Part 6 長文穴埋め問題 ···

Questions 1-4 refer to the following email.

To: All staff
From: Sarah Blanch
Re: Lateness

------. If you are one of these people, then please ignore this email. If not, read on. It has
  1.
been ------ to my attention that several members of staff have been tardy in arriving at
   2.
work. I would like to remind these people that regular office hours are from 9 a.m. to
5 p.m. This means that you need to be sitting at your desks by 9 a.m. It does not mean
arriving at 9:00 before ------ into the bathroom to get ready for the working day.
    3.
Next year, we will be starting a flexitime working schedule that will enable you to arrive
at a time of your choosing between 9 a.m. and 11 a.m. and to leave later than current
regulations allow. This will enable those of you who are night owls to come in later. ------
    4.
then, however, please be reminded that office rules mean that you must be here, ready to
start work, at 9 a.m. sharp.

---

1. (A) Some staff members have been
leaving the office early.
   (B) We are introducing a flexitime system
next week
   (C) I know many of you arrive at the
office on time.
   (D) From today, office hours are 9 a.m. to
5 p.m.

2 (A) brought
   (B) announced
   (C) informed
   (D) carried

3. (A) disappear
   (B) disappeared
   (C) will disappear
   (D) disappearing

4. (A) Until
   (B) By
   (C) After
   (D) Through

例題

Car rental

Roberta Jacobs: Hi, I'm flying to Liverpool for a conference, and I have two days free afterwards. I was hoping to rent a car after the conference ends and drive out to the Lake District. It's always been a dream of mine to visit Peter Rabbit country. Since it's in the countryside, there are few trains.   Can anyone recommend a good car hire company?

　　　　Clair Simmonds: I used Easyrent last year. They met me at the airport to take me to their office and the cars were new and in good condition. The prices are reasonable.

　　　　Jeff Harwood: I always use Easyrent. I have found their prices fair, with no charge added for an extra driver.

レンタカーが必要な理由

お勧めのレンタカー会社名とその理由(送迎、車の状態、価格)

お勧めのレンタカーショップ名とその理由(価格、追加料金なし)

To: Easyrent
From: Roberta Jacobs
Subject: Car rental

Dear Sir or Madam,
I am looking for a small car to rent for two days over the weekend from June 10th to June 11th. Ideally, I would pick it up on Saturday morning but if you are not open on Saturdays then I am prepared to pick it up on Friday evening before you close. I would like to return it by 8:00 pm on Sunday, but will return it in the afternoon if that time is too late. I have minimal luggage so only need a small car and will be using local roads only. Could you recommend a car for me?

Regards,
Roberta Jacobs

顧客の希望 (車のタイプ、日時、期間)

顧客の許容範囲 (車の受け取りと返却日時)

顧客の希望(車のタイプ、使用目的)

Your booking details	Details	Price
Pick-up: Liverpool office Saturday June 10th (from 8:00 am) ◀	Car type: Small hybrid, automatic ◀ Fuel: Full tank, fill on return	Basic price for two days: £200 Insurance: £10/day Tax: 10% of total (not included in charge) ◀
Drop-off: Liverpool office Sunday June 11th (by 8:00 pm) ◀	Transport to and from airport: Free shuttle bus ◀	Charge for extra driver: None

車のタイプ
受け取り日時
料金
送迎
返却日時

Q1. Why does Roberta Jacobs want to rent a car?

(A) She is going to a conference.
(B) She wants to visit a particular area.
(C) The train system in that country is poor.
(D) She wants to see wild rabbits.

Q2. What aspect of Easyrent was NOT mentioned?

(A) The office is a short walk from the airport.
(B) The vehicles are well maintained.
(C) An extra driver can be added.
(D) The prices are not too high.

Q3. When does Roberta most want to rent the car?

(A) From Friday evening to Sunday evening
(B) From Saturday morning to Monday morning
(C) From Saturday morning to Sunday evening
(D) From Saturday afternoon to Sunday afternoon

Q4. What kind of car does she request?

(A) A large car with plenty of room for luggage
(B) A small car that is fast enough for highways
(C) A car that needs little gasoline
(D) A compact car that is good for narrow roads

Q5. How much will Roberta pay in total?

(A) £202
(B) £220
(C) £242
(D) £255

ここがポイント！ 文章と表を用いて手配や手続きを正確に実行しよう

　メールやチャットの文章と表やリスト、スケジュールや旅程表といった英文素材を組み合わせて、手配や手続きを正確に行ない、変更が必要な場合は適切に変更できるか、という設定も読解問題に頻繁に登場します。航空券の手配、レンタカーの申し込み、バスのチャーターといった交通手段に関係するもの、イベント会場やホテル、レストランの予約、プレゼンテーション順の変更などが多いようです。文章の中にある条件や要望と表などの中の情報を照らして正確に読む必要があります。

　例題では、1つ目のチャットで、レンタカーが必要になった Roberta に、Clair と Jeff がお勧めのレンタカー会社とその理由を伝えています。次に、Roberta が2人の提案どおり Easyrent に、借りたい車のタイプや日時、期間を伝えるメールを送り、最後に、予約の詳細が表にまとめられ、Roberta の希望通りの予約が正確にできていることがわかります。

例題の正解

Q1 (B)　Q2 (A)　Q3 (C)　Q4 (D)　Q5 (C)

最重要ヴォキャブラリー　🔊 43　🔊 44

- [ ] **baggage** [bǽgidʒ] 名「かばん」「手荷物」　baggage claim [bǽgidʒ kléim] と言うと、空港などの「預入手荷物引取所」のこと。

- [ ] **boarding** [bɔ́ːrdiŋ] 名「搭乗」　boarding pass「搭乗券」、boarding gate「搭乗口」という表現も TOEIC では頻出。関連語に board [bɔ́ːrd] 動「搭乗する」名「役員」「重役」がある。

- [ ] **departure** [dipáːrtʃər] 名「出発」　反意語は arrival [əráivəl]「到着」。それぞれの動詞は、depart [dipáːrt]「出発する」と arrive [əráiv]「到着する」で、TOEIC では、空港や駅、移動に関する文脈で頻出。

- [ ] **gain** [géin] 名「増加」「利益」動「獲得する」「増す」「価値が上がる」　「利益」の意味の反意語は loss [lɔ́ːs]「損失」。「獲得する」の意味の同意語に get、反意語に lose「失う」があり、「価値が上がる」の意味の同意語は rise、反意語は fall「価値が下がる」。

- [ ] **hedge** [hédʒ] 名「垣根」「保険」動「生け垣で囲う」「(丸損を防ぐために)保険をかける」　TOEIC では、経済用語としてほぼ「保険」「保険をかける」という意味で用いられる。

- [ ] **invest** [invést] 動「投資する」　名詞は investment [invéstmənt]「投資」。「〜に投資する」は invest in 〜と言い、make an investment in 〜もほぼ同意である。

- [ ] **luggage** [lʌ́gidʒ] 名「かばん」「手荷物」　同意語に baggage がある。どちらも不可算名詞で、複数形にならないことに注意。TOEIC では bag などと言い換えられることがある。

- [ ] **minimal** [mínəməl] 形「(費用・損害等が)最小の」「ごく小さい」「微細な」　関連語に、minimum [mínəməm] 形「最小の」「最低の」名「最小限度」「最小量」がある。

- [ ] **particular** [pərtíkjulər] 形「特別の」「特定の」名「詳細」　「特定の」の意味の反意語は general [dʒénərəl]「一般的な」。副詞は particularly [pərtíkjulərli]「特に」である。

- [ ] **share** [ʃéər] 名「株」「取り分」動「共有する」　「株」の意味の同意語に stock [stɔ́k] がある。shareholder [ʃéər hòuldər] は「株主」のことで、meeting of shareholders と言うと「株主総会」を意味する。

Let's Try

Part 7 読解問題 ···

Questions 1-5 refer to the following email, boarding pass, and itinerary.

Hi Ali,

I've arranged your flight schedule for Tokyo to Wilmington, North Carolina, as follows. Your flight from Tokyo leaves at 9:00 am, so you need to leave your hotel in Shinjuku, Tokyo by 6:30. I'm sorry it's so early, but you need to leave extra time for international flights. It's recommended that you arrive at the airport three hours before the flight, but I think two hours will be enough. As you know, there are no direct flights from Tokyo to Wilmington, North Carolina, so you'll be changing at Dallas. In the U.S., you have to collect your baggage at the point of entry into the country—which will be Dallas, not Wilmington—and then put your baggage through security once again. This is why I gave you extra time at Dallas. You will have two hours between landing in Dallas and boarding the next plane to Wilmington. Have a great trip!

John

Boarding Pass

Name of passenger: Ali Scrimbles

From: Dallas, Texas

To: Wilmington, N. Carolina

Gate **45**

Gate closes 40 minutes before departure

Boarding at
11:30

Date:
March 15

Seat **13A**

Conference Schedule at North Carolina University

Date	Talk	Speaker
March 16th AM	Investing for the future: picking the best stocks for the next five years	Ali Scrimbles
PM	The habits of effective CEOs	Beverly Chin
March 17th AM	How to survive a downturn: hedging against risk	Ali Scrimbles
PM	Maintaining strong social networks for business success	Beverly Chin

1. Why does Ali need to leave the hotel so early?
   (A) It takes a long time to get to the airport.
   (B) He must arrive at the airport three hours early.
   (C) The traffic is very slow after 6:30 am.
   (D) He is taking an international flight.

2. What does Ali have to do at Dallas Airport?
   (A) Wait for the plane to take off again
   (B) Wait in the transit lounge
   (C) Rush to catch a connecting flight
   (D) Repeat the security process

3. What time will Ali's plane arrive in Dallas?
   (A) 9:30
   (B) 10:10
   (C) 11:30
   (D) 12:10

4. In the conference schedule, the word "downturn" is closest in meaning to
   (A) recession
   (B) break time
   (C) danger
   (D) security

5. What topic is Ali probably an expert on?
   (A) Making good business connections
   (B) Buying shares to make a profit
   (C) Developing one's personality for success
   (D) Taking risks to make huge gains

Unit ⓬

文法編 ……〔代名詞〕

例題

Ms. Nelson led safety inspections at the production facility in Toronto with three of _____ colleagues.

 (A)　her   (B)　herself   (C)　she   (D)　hers

ここがポイント！　名詞の＜数＞と＜性別＞、代名詞の＜文中での働き＞に注意！

　同じ名詞を繰り返し使うことを避けるために、英語では代名詞が多く使われます。いくつかの種類がありますが、TOEIC で出題されるのは主に、前に出てきた人や物事に関係する名詞の代わりをする人称代名詞です。前出の名詞の単数・複数や男性・女性の違い、主語なのか、目的語なのか、といった文の中での代名詞の役割によって用いる代名詞は決まります。

　上の問題では、Ms. Nelson という女性が、「彼女の」同僚とともに検査をしたと理解するのが自然です。「彼女の」という所有格の代名詞は her ですので、(A) が空欄には適当です。

正解　(A)

問題文の訳：ネルソンさんは、トロントの製造施設の安全検査を 3 人の同僚とともに行った。

　人称代名詞について、前出の名詞の意味と代名詞の文中での働きをまとめます。

名詞の意味 ＼ 文中での働き	主格 （〜は、〜が）	所有格 （〜の）	目的格 （〜を、〜に）	所有代名詞 （〜のもの）	再帰代名詞 （〜自身）
「私」	I	my	me	mine	myself
「あなた」	you	your	you	yours	yourself
「彼」	he	his	him	his	himself
「彼女」	she	her	her	hers	herself
「私たち」	we	our	us	ours	ourselves
「あなたたち」	you	your	you	yours	yourselves
「彼ら、彼女たち、それら」	they	their	them	theirs	themselves
「それ」	it	its	it	———	itself

以下に、人称代名詞に関する注意すべき点を挙げておきます。

ポイント1　目的格と再帰代名詞の違い

　この 2 つは混同しやすく、区別しにくいかもしれませんが、下の例文を見るとわかりやすいでしょう。
  Mr. Suzuki talked to **him**.　← 鈴木氏が（誰か他の）男性に話しかけた。
  Mr. Suzuki talked to **himself**.　← 鈴木氏が、自分自身に話しかけた、つまり独り言を言った。

ポイント2　「前出の名詞」の有無について

　前に出てきた人や物事に関係する名詞の代わりをするのが人称代名詞、と説明しましたが、必ず代名詞よりも前に名詞があるわけではありません。後にある場合や、明記されていない場合もあります。後者のケースでは、前後の状況や文脈から何を指しているのかを判断する必要があります。

後にあるケース：

While **she** was walking along the street, Ms. Kim got a phone call from her client.

← 前出の she は、後ろの Ms. Kim を指している。

It is obvious that we can't meet the deadline.　← It は後の that 以下全体を指している。

明記されていない例：

The guide will provide **you** with an information package.

← 「ガイドが様々な情報が入った袋を**あなた方に**渡します」という状況であると判断できる。

Please be sure that **your** child has a signed letter of parental consent.

← 「確実に～してください」と依頼している相手は「あなた＝ you」なので、「**あなたの**子ども」のことを依頼していると判断できる。

最重要ヴォキャブラリー　🔊45 🔊46

☐ **administer** [ædmínistər] 動「**管理する**」「**運営する**」「**実施する**」　名詞は administration [ædmìnəstréiʃən]「政権」「管理」「経営陣」「実施」と、administrator [ædmínəstreitər]「管理者」、形容詞は administrative [ædmínəstrèitiv]「管理の」「経営の」。

☐ **allocate** [ǽləkèit] 動「**～に割り当てる**」「**計上する**」　allocate A to B で「A（資金や責任など）を B（人など）に割り当てる」という意味の表現。名詞は allocation [ǽləkéiʃən]「割り当て」「配分」である。

☐ **apprentice** [əpréntis] 名「**見習い**」「**実習生**」　apprenticeship と言うと、「見習いの身分」や「見習い期間」を意味する。

☐ **concern** [kənsə́:rn] 名「**関心**」「**心配事**」 動「**関係する**」「**関心を持つ**」「**心配している**」　To whom it may concern は「関係各位」「ご担当者様」という意味で、推薦状や証明書など公式な手紙の冒頭に使う慣用表現である。

☐ **consent** [kənsént] 名「**承諾**」「**合意**」動「**承諾する**」　「承諾」の意味では、同意語に permission [pərmíʃən]がある。by common consent は「満場一致で」、by mutual consent は「双方合意の上で」という意味。

☐ **implementation** [ìmpləməntéiʃən] 名「**実施**」「**履行**」　関連語に、implement [ímpləmènt] 動「実施する」「履行する」/ [ímpləmənt] 名「道具」がある。

☐ **involve** [inválv] 動「**含む**」「**関係する**」　名詞は involvement [inválvmənt]「関与」である。

☐ **majority** [mədʒɔ́:rəti] 名「**大多数**」「**過半数**」　単独で用いる場合、通常単数扱いし、動詞は単数形に合わせる。the majority of ～「～の大多数」と言う場合、動詞は of の後ろの名詞の単複に合わせる。反意語は minority [minɔ́:rəti]「少数派」「少数民族」。

☐ **meantime** [mí:ntàim, mì:ntáim] 名「**合間**」　in the meantime「その間に」という表現で使われることが多い。

☐ **outlet** [áutlet] 名「**販売店**」「**はけ口**」「**コンセント**」　factory outlet と言うと「工場直営店」、retail outlet は「小売店」のこと。

☐ **routinely** [rù:tí:nli] 副「**日常的に**」「**決まって**」　形容詞は routine [ru:tí:n]「日常的な」「決まりきった」、名詞も routine で「日課」「お決まりの出し物」。

☐ **ultimately** [ʌ́ltəmətli] 副「**最終的に**」「**結局**」　形容詞は、ultimate [ʌ́ltəmət]「最終的な」「最高の」である。

☐ **vary** [véəri] 動「**変わる**」「**変える**」　関連語に、形容詞の varied [véərid]「変化に富んだ」「多様な」、various [véəriəs]「様々な」、名詞の variety [vəráiəti]「多様性」「種類」、variation [vèəriéiʃən]「変化」「差異」がある。

☐ **voter** [vóutər] 名「**投票者**」「**有権者**」　voter turnout と言うと「投票率」のこと。関連語に、vote [vóut] 動「投票する」名「票」「投票」がある。

Let's Try

Part 5 短文穴埋め問題 ··

1. Company accountants have been working more efficiently since _____ began using the new software.

(A) their

(B) them

(C) they

(D) themselves

2. Our competitor's new line of copiers is both cheaper and faster than _____ .

(A) us

(B) our

(C) ourselves

(D) ours

3. Ms. Rogers checked the contents of all boxes in the warehouse before distributing _____ to the retail outlets.

(A) her

(B) them

(C) it

(D) him

4. According to the survey, the majority of voters said the state of the economy was _____ greatest concern.

(A) they

(B) their

(C) it

(D) its

5. The supervisors routinely administer tests to employees to confirm _____ knowledge of the company's procedures.

(A) their

(B) them

(C) themselves

(D) they

Unit 1
Unit 2
Unit 3
Unit 4
Unit 5
Unit 6
Unit 7
Unit 8
Unit 9
Unit 10
Unit 11
Unit 12

Questions 1-4 refer to the following information.

The CEO, or Chief Executive Officer, holds the highest position in any company.
CEOs are ------- the managerial decisions of a company as well as its performance and the
1.
implementation of short- and long-term plans. ------- . She or he allocates tasks to -------
2.   3.
including the CFO (Chief Finance Officer), the CTO (Chief Technical Officer), and the
COO (Chief Operating Officer).
The degree to which a CEO is concerned with the details of a company will vary depending
on its size. In a major established company, the CEO focuses more on the key decisions that
need to be taken while the CEO of a startup has ------- in every aspect of the organization.
4.

1. (A) responsible for ultimately
   (B) ultimately responsible for
   (C) for responsible ultimately
   (D) responsible for the ultimate

2. (A) Surprisingly, a CEO does not always
       have the highest position.
   (B) Of course, a CEO cannot undertake so
       many responsibilities alone.
   (C) In the meantime, the CEO must
       distribute work among secretaries.
   (D) After all, the CEO is the only major
       officer in a company.

3 (A) apprentices
   (B) juniors
   (C) subordinates
   (D) trainees

4 (A) being involved
   (B) be involved
   (C) to be as involved
   (D) to be involved

読解編 ·····〔Triple Passages 3〕

例題

Notice of Closure

Salsa Suppers will be closing at the end of this month, on March 31st. Over the last few years, the number of visitors to the city center has declined as shoppers increasingly visited the out-of-town Newmarket Shopping Mall. But do not despair! In three months' time, we will be opening a new restaurant, The Trip to Mexico, in that same shopping mall. The new venue will offer more space for us to cook and more seating for you, our customers, so please support us in our new venture. Before we begin, our chefs are taking an extended trip to Mexico to learn the secrets of Mexican cooking from some of Mexico's top chefs. We hope that you will appreciate the addition of exciting new dishes to the established classics of Salsa Suppers. We look forward to seeing you all in the summer. Adios!

タイトルと1文目:
Salsa Suppers の閉店

[Over the last few years...Newmarket Shopping Mall]
閉店理由

[In three months' time…that same shopping mall] 後継店の名前と場所

Restaurant reviews I was saddened to hear of the closure of Salsa Suppers, the restaurant with hot Latin flavors and cocktails that just blew me away. It was the perfect Friday night hangout. I searched for another restaurant that is just as good, and after a few months, I found it! The Trip to Mexico, owned by the same people as Salsa Suppers is even better than its predecessor. The flavors are just as good, the cocktails better, and the seating is even more comfortable than before. I thoroughly recommend it. One disappointing aspect is the location. The Newmarket Shopping Mall is convenient, I'm sure, but it lacks atmosphere. Never mind. Once you step inside The Trip to Mexico, you will forget everything except what lies within the four walls of the restaurant.

[The Trip to Mexico … recommend it] 両レストランの比較

[The Newmarket Shopping Mall … lacks atmosphere] 新店舗があるモールの欠点

New Shopping Center Proves Popular

Since the Newmarket Shopping Mall opened, small businesses that were formerly located in the city centre have been moving to this out-of-town mecca, where hundreds of stores have been brought together in a rural setting with plenty of parking. This is very convenient for the shopper, who no longer has to walk from shop to shop to find daily necessities and a nice café, but there has been a negative effect as well. The city center is now dying as shoppers stay away. This phenomenon is not confined to this town: it is happening all over the country where similar developments are taking place. City planners need to take this into account when they create future shopping malls.

Q1. Why is the Salsa Suppers restaurant closing?

(A) Fewer visitors are coming to the area.
(B) The restaurant has gone bankrupt.
(C) It is moving to another country.
(D) A highway will be built in its location.

Q2. What will the restaurant staff do in Mexico?

(A) Interview and hire some top chefs
(B) Take a vacation before starting again
(C) Study the local cooking of the region
(D) Open a new branch of the restaurant

Q3. In the restaurant review, "blew me away" in line 3 is closest in meaning to

(A) Gave me a headache
(B) Impressed me
(C) Made ma laugh
(D) Disappointed me

Q4. What is a disappointing aspect of The Trip to Mexico?

(A) It is not comfortable.
(B) The cocktails are dull.
(C) It is inconvenient to get to.
(D) The location lacks atmosphere.

Q5. According to the articles, what should city planners do?

(A) Provide a lot of parking spaces for shoppers.
(B) Consider the effects of shopping malls on city centers.
(C) Ban out-of-town shopping malls completely.
(D) Make sure that shopping malls include nice cafes.

ここがポイント！ 知っておきたい「1つの事象について書かれた複数の文書」という組み合わせ

triple passages の出題パターンの1つに、3つのうちの2つ、またはすべての文書で1つの事柄について論じるものがあります。形式は、報告書や評論が多く、内容は、ある会社の業績や新しい経営方針、経営陣人事、市場の動向といったビジネスに関するものから、最近私たちの生活の中に浸透してきた、商品やサービスについての消費者のレビューなどがあります。表やグラフのような視覚的情報が含まれているものは比較的取り組みやすいですが、文字情報ばかりの場合は、敬遠したい気持ちになる素材です。しかし、タイトルや最初の部分を見て、同じ表現や類似表現がある場合には、1つの事象について書かれた複数の文書なのでは？と推測をしてみてください。それぞれの文書のおおまかな内容や関係性がつかめると、気持ちの上で余裕をもって設問に取り組めるようになるはずです。

例題では、1つ目の文書の Notice of Closure「閉店のお知らせ」というタイトルと1文目 Salsa Suppers will be closing at the end of this month…「サルサ・サパーズは今月末で閉店」、2つ目の文書の1文目 I was saddened to hear of the closure of Salsa Suppers…「サルサ・サパーズが閉店と聞いて悲しい」の部分から、レストランの閉店について書かれた2つの文書なのでは？と推測できます。また、最初の2つの文書には、Salsa Suppers の他にも the Newmarket Shopping Mall、The Trip to Mexico という表現が共通していて、3つ目の文書にも the Newmarket Shopping Mall という表現があります。3つのキーワードをもとに、それぞれの関係性、筆者の考えや主張を正しく読み取ることが求められています。

例題の正解

Q1 (A)　Q2 (C)　Q3 (B)　Q4 (D)　Q5 (B)

最重要ヴォキャブラリー 🔊 47 🔊 48

☐ **ban** [bǽn] 動「禁止する」名「禁止」「禁止令」　動詞の同意語に prohibit [prouhíbit] がある。lift a ban と言うと「解禁する」、impose a ban は「禁止する」という意味。

☐ **bankrupt** [bǽŋkrʌpt] 形「破産した」　go bankrupt で「破産する」。名詞は bankruptcy [bǽŋkrʌptsi]「破産」「倒産」で、declare bankruptcy と言うと「破産宣告する」。

☐ **confine** [kənfáin] 動「～に限定する」「閉じ込める」　not be confined to ～で「～に限ったものではない」という意味の表現。「～に限定する」の同意語に restrict [ristríkt] がある。

☐ **contain** [kəntéin] 動「含む」　container [kəntéinər] と言えば「容器」のこと。

☐ **decline** [dikláin] 動「断る」「衰える」「減少する」名「衰退」　「断る」の意味の類義語に、reject [ridʒékt]、refuse [rifjúːz]、turn down、「減少する」の意味の類義語に、decrease [dikríːs]、reduce [ridjúːs]、drop などがある。

☐ **despair** [dispéər] 動「絶望する」名「絶望」「失望」　「～に絶望する」「～を諦める」と言うときには、despair of [at、over] ～で表現する。

☐ **extend** [iksténd] 動「延長する」「延期する」「広がる」　名詞の extension [iksténʃən]「（期間の）延長」「内線番号」「増築部分」「拡張」とともに多義語で、どの意味でも TOEIC に頻出。

☐ **pharmacy** [fɑ́ːrməsi] 名「薬局」「製薬会社」　「製薬会社」という意味では pharmaceutical [fɑ̀ːrməsúːtikəl] company とも言う。pharmacist [fɑ́ːrməsist] は「薬剤師」。

☐ **physician** [fiziʃən] 名「医師」「内科医」　「医師」の意味では、doctor と言い換えられる。関連語に、surgeon [sə́ːrdʒən]「外科医」がある。

☐ **predecessor** [prédəsèsər] 名「前任者」「先輩」　反意語は、successor [səksésər]「後任」「後継者」である。

☐ **relieve** [rilíːv] 動「（苦痛などを）和らげる」「～を取り除く」　名詞は relief [rilíːf]「安心」「緩和」「救

済」で、What a relief! は「これで安心だ」という意味の表現。

☐ **remedy** [rémədi] 图**「改善策」「医薬品」「治療」** 「改善策」の意味では solution [səlú:ʃən]、「医薬品」の意味では medicine [médəsin] や drug と言い換え可能。

☐ **suggestion** [səgdʒéstʃən] 图**「提案」** 同意語に proposal [prəpóuzəl] がある。make a suggestion と言うと、動詞の suggest [səgdʒést]「提案する」とほぼ同意。

☐ **thoroughly** [θə́:rouli] 副**「徹底的に」** 発音とアクセントの位置に注意。同意語は completely [kəmplí:tli]、形容詞は thorough [θə́:rou]「徹底的な」である。

Let's Try

Part 7 読解問題 ···

Questions 1-5 refer to the following text messages, medicine instructions and review.

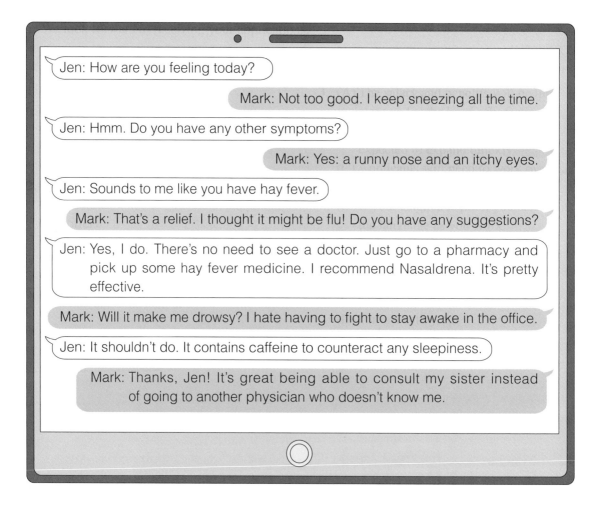

Jen: How are you feeling today?

Mark: Not too good. I keep sneezing all the time.

Jen: Hmm. Do you have any other symptoms?

Mark: Yes: a runny nose and an itchy eyes.

Jen: Sounds to me like you have hay fever.

Mark: That's a relief. I thought it might be flu! Do you have any suggestions?

Jen: Yes, I do. There's no need to see a doctor. Just go to a pharmacy and pick up some hay fever medicine. I recommend Nasaldrena. It's pretty effective.

Mark: Will it make me drowsy? I hate having to fight to stay awake in the office.

Jen: It shouldn't do. It contains caffeine to counteract any sleepiness.

Mark: Thanks, Jen! It's great being able to consult my sister instead of going to another physician who doesn't know me.

NASALDRENA: Instructions

Who can use this product	Do NOT use this product
• Children 12 years and over • Adults	• for children under 12 years of age • if foil seal is broken
Use this product for	**How to use this product**
Rapid relief from the symptoms of hayfever and year-round allergies without causing drowsiness. One daily dose provides relief from sneezing, runny nose, and itchy eyes.	Take one tablet per day after a meal

Nasaldrena ★★★★★

I have tried many hay fever remedies over the years but none of them worked well. Some were simply ineffective; others fixed my hay fever but made me so drowsy that the boss would catch me sleeping at my desk. Finally, I've found a remedy that works! It contains antihistamines, which do make you drowsy, but also contains caffeine to counteract the drowsiness. Just be careful not to have too many coffees during the day, or you won't sleep at night! I can thoroughly recommend this product.

Mark Jacobs

1. What is Mark's problem?
   (A) He has a pollen allergy.
   (B) He has caught flu.
   (C) He keeps falling asleep.
   (D) He has a blocked nose.

2. Who is Jen?
   (A) Mark's mother
   (B) A doctor
   (C) A pharmacist
   (D) A spouse

3. Who should NOT use this medicine?
   (A) Young adults
   (B) People with allergies
   (C) Young children
   (D) People with itchy noses

4. In the instructions, the word "drowsiness" is closest in meaning to
   (A) Itchiness
   (B) Sadness
   (C) Short temper
   (D) Sleepiness

5. Why does the medicine contain caffeine?
   (A) To help the taker stay awake
   (B) To relieve the symptoms
   (C) To improve the flavor
   (D) To help the taker work hard

Unit 1 Unit 2 Unit 3 Unit 4 Unit 5 Unit 6 Unit 7 Unit 8 Unit 9 Unit 10 Unit 11 Unit 12

最重要ヴォキャブラリー索引

各 Unit の **最重要ヴォキャブラリー** コーナーで取り上げた語彙の索引です。アルファベット順に配列しています。数字は、掲載されているページを示しています。

著　者

古家　聡（ふるや　さとる）　武蔵野大学グローバル学部グローバルコミュニケーション学科教授

藤岡美香子（ふじおか　みかこ）　東海大学経営学部観光ビジネス学科講師

Geoffrey TOZER（ジェフリー　トーザー）　創価大学非常勤講師

TOEIC® L&R TEST リーディング&ヴォキャブラリー徹底演習

2021 年 2 月 20 日　第 1 版発行
2024 年 3 月 20 日　第 6 版発行

著　　者 —— 古家　聡／藤岡美香子／ Geoffrey TOZER
発 行 者 —— 前田俊秀
発 行 所 —— 株式会社　三修社
　　　　　　〒 150-0001　東京都渋谷区神宮前 2-2-22
　　　　　　TEL 03-3405-4511　　FAX 03-3405-4522
　　　　　　振替 00190-9-72758
　　　　　　https://www.sanshusha.co.jp
　　　　　　編集担当 三井るり子
印 刷 所 —— 広研印刷株式会社

READING AND VOCABULARY TRAINING FOR THE TOEIC® L&R TEST
©Satoru FURUYA, Mikako FUJIOKA and Geoffrey TOZER
2021 Printed in Japan　ISBN978-4-384-33503-3 C1082

表紙デザイン —— 峯岸孝之
本 文 Ｄ Ｔ Ｐ —— 有限会社トライアングル
準拠音声録音 —— ELEC
準拠音声製作 —— 高速録音株式会社

教科書準拠 CD 発売
本書の準拠 CD をご希望の方は弊社までお問い合わせください。